Copyright

Healed & Whole or Wounded & Broken: Which One Are You

This book is presented for educational, informational, and inspirational purposes only. The views and opinions expressed herein are those of the author and are not intended to replace professional medical, psychological, legal, financial, or counseling advice. Readers are encouraged to seek qualified professional assistance when appropriate.

Scripture quotations, unless otherwise indicated, are taken from the Holy Bible. Any emphasis within Scripture quotations has been added by the author.

The stories, examples, and illustrations contained in this book are intended to convey spiritual and life principles. In some cases, names, identifying details, and circumstances may have been changed to protect privacy.

Printed in the United States of America.

For information regarding speaking engagements, ministry opportunities, coaching, or bulk book orders, contact:

The Outstanding Man Enterprises LLC

Email: ***INFORMATION@TOMENTERPRISESLLC.COM***

Follow LARRY BOBO on social media and “Like” and “Comment” on content and what you’re about to read.

@therealmroutstanding

@therealmroutstanding

Larry Bobo

@_larrybobo

@Larry_Bobo

Table of Contents

Acknowledgment

I'd like to thank my pastors, Otha and LaRonna Turnbough for their obedience in starting the ministry God called them to. I've seen several ministries over the years and been part of many as well. I've served in multiple capacities and have experienced it all. My spiritual journey has been an amazing one that God has definitely directed my path.

I've grown in ways I could never have imagined. Each one of those ministries served a purpose in my spiritual journey and I was able to take something away from each. And now I have come to a place in these end times that has brought all that I have learned, full circle.

A ministry that has made it make sense and answered so many questions and confirmed the revelations I've had over the years. It has also confirmed the feelings I've had in my spirit for years about so many things and brought about understanding, knowledge and wisdom. Unlike most ministries, this is unique in that there is no fleecing of members, no sexual perversion behind closed doors and a pastor who is transparent, vulnerable and lives spiritually clean.

One of his gifts is pulling out things in scripture that most overlook or are scared to teach on, and his boldness. And he has been given an ability to empower those he teaches to fully and truly walk in invincibility in the spirit and defeat someone we can't even see. The way God intended.

It's not a light topical message or cruise ship type of atmosphere. It's a battle ship that's engaging and thought provoking using scripture right from the Word. It's not a feel good message or performance to come for one day a week and go live hypocritically the other 6.

It's a true full gospel ministry that focuses on dream interpretation, healing of the sick, speaking in tongue, demonic deliverance and prophetic word. What Jesus told us to do. Empowering Believers to truly live clean and in the invincible state God intended when He said "let them have dominion."

As the Bible says, obedience is better than sacrifice. Therefore I am humbled, grateful and thankful for their obedience and dedication to starting and patiently waiting on God to grow what He ordained before the beginning.

It is because of that ministry, I can truly say, I am empowered to walk this spiritual journey literally with no fear and with the knowledge and understanding of how to recognize and battle the enemy toe to toe and win, every time.

Introduction

Being single in today's world can be hard. Dating, discerning intentions, building connections, and trying to find a wife can become emotionally exhausting. What made it even more difficult for me was not just the process itself, but the repeated pattern I kept encountering along the way. I met several women, and in many of those encounters, I found myself face to face with women who were wounded, guarded, and emotionally disconnected, yet many of them did not seem to realize how deeply broken they were. They resisted outside perspective, rejected correction, struggled with emotional connection, and before long, the relationship would begin to unravel, mostly before it ever got started good.

After a while, I began to question myself. I wondered if I was somehow attracting wounded individuals, or if maybe something was wrong with me. There is an old saying that you often attract what you are, and that thought weighed heavily on me. But I had already gone through my own process of inner healing and deliverance multiple times. I believed I had come through some of the deepest valleys of my life and had reached a place of greater healing and wholeness. So I kept asking myself the same question: if I had done the work, if I had faced my pain, if I had allowed God to heal me, then why did I keep crossing paths with people who seemed so deeply broken?

In one conversation, a good friend of mine, someone I consider spiritually grounded and discerning, offered a thought that stayed with me. They suggested that perhaps this was connected to purpose. Maybe, they said, some of these individuals were crossing my path so their eyes could be opened to their brokenness, it was my ministry. Maybe what I kept experiencing was not just frustration, but revelation. That thought sat with me too. Then, after more reflection and research, I came to a startling conclusion: as much as 75% of the world's population is currently broken and 100% were broken at some point in their childhood. That means three out of every four people on this earth are carrying some level of unresolved heart wounds, childhood trauma, emotional fragmentation, or inner instability and brokenness. Once that reality settled into my spirit, it changed how I saw people, relationships, and the dating world altogether.

What I once thought was an unusual pattern in my personal life began to look more like a painful truth about the condition of humanity. Brokenness is not rare. It is common. It is hidden behind smiles, confidence, accomplishments, humor, beauty, ambition, charm, religion, routine and mainly, pride. Many people function every day without ever realizing how much of their life has been shaped by wounds they never addressed. They have learned how to survive, how to cope, how to perform, and how to adapt, but they have not truly healed. And because they have not healed, their pain eventually begins to speak through their choices, their fears, their reactions, their relationships, and their inability to receive healthy love.

That truth became intensely personal for me when I entered a relationship and fell in love with someone who would eventually break my heart. That experience became a turning point. It forced me to stop looking at brokenness as just a pattern I was noticing in others and to confront it as a painful reality with real consequences. Like so many others, I learned firsthand that hurt people hurt people. Not always because they are malicious. Not always because they intend to destroy. But because unhealed pain has a way of spilling onto the people who get close enough to love them including their children.

That relationship opened my eyes in a way nothing else had before. I realized it was not necessarily that I was drawing broken people to me. It was that brokenness is everywhere. I had simply fallen in love during one of those encounters, and for the first time, the cost of another person's unhealed wounds reached my own heart deeply enough to change me. That pain became a lens. It showed me how many people are trying to give love, receive love, and build relationships while still carrying old grief, old trauma, old fear, old disappointments, soul-ties and old survival patterns that have never truly been healed or even addressed.

There were signs long before our relationship fell apart. They were not signs of evil in the dramatic sense. They were signs of deep emotional exhaustion, unresolved pain, and a heart that had learned to protect itself at all costs. At first, I interpreted many of those signs as personality quirks, communication differences, or emotional preferences. But over time, I began to understand that I was witnessing what happens when a person wants love but has not healed enough to safely receive it.

One of the first things she told me, as she chuckled was, 'I can't be delivered,' which was a demonic influence speaking through her. It was at that moment, I fully understood that this was going to be a real spiritual fight, if we were to be together, because of the spiritual stronghold present. I also heard the voice of someone who had lived with pain for so long that wholeness felt foreign. I heard someone who had survived, but not healed. And there is a difference.

I remember the way she treated her only son, though the full revelation didn't come until after we stopped dating. She didn't treat him the same way she treated her other children. At the time, he was still trying to find his direction in life and she seemingly had given up on him because in her eyes, he wasn't doing anything with his life — even though he wasn't yet thirty years old.

What I later realized was that he looked exactly like her father, his grandfather, who had passed away some years earlier. She had shown me old photographs and often said how much he resembled his grandfather like a twin. In time, it became clear to me that the way she treated her son was deeply connected to unresolved pain from the relationship she wanted and never had with her father. Every time she looked at her son, she was reminded of the hurt, disappointment, and emotional absence she carried for years. Instead of seeing him for who he was, she unconsciously saw the wounds attached to the man he resembled.

As time went on, I saw more clearly how unhealed pain can shape the way a person thinks, responds, and connects. Reflection and accountability felt threatening to her. Emotional clarity was difficult. Questions about love, growth, healing, or past lessons or accountability often led to defensiveness rather than openness. She avoided taking any responsibility for failure of past marriages, either blaming her ex's or deflecting. There were moments when I could see softness underneath the surface, moments when I could tell that something tender still existed behind the walls. But the walls eventually returned. She wanted love, but closeness felt unsafe. She wanted reassurance but struggled to trust it when it came. She desired connection, but feared the vulnerability required to sustain it. She used to say to me in the beginning that I was controlling or I was selfish but she soon realized I wasn't. I'm not sure if she ever realized she was judging me based on past experiences versus being submerged in the moment and enjoying and appreciating how I actually treated her.

One of the clearest signs of a wounded and broken person is what happens when truth confronts the areas of their life they have worked hard to avoid. They become defensive and confrontational.

Many people carry emotional, spiritual, and relational wounds that have never been fully addressed. These wounds often reveal themselves through recurring behaviors, unhealthy relationship patterns, emotional triggers, and defensive reactions. Scripture reminds us that "Above all else, guard your heart, for everything you do flows from it" (Proverbs 4:23). A healthy heart is not one protected by walls, bitterness, denial or unforgiveness but one that is continually healed and renewed.

When unresolved issues are gently confronted, some individuals become defensive rather than reflective. Instead of considering whether there may be truth in the observation, they may perceive concern as criticism or accountability as judgment. The conversation quickly shifts from examining the wound to protecting it.

What often stands out is not the disagreement itself that they are broken, but the intensity of the reaction. Healthy and emotionally mature people are generally willing to examine themselves, even when the truth is uncomfortable. They possess the humility to ask, "Could there be something here that I need to address?" Wounded people, however, frequently interpret any discussion of unresolved pain and brokenness as a personal attack and judgement.

Many of these reactions can be traced back to childhood experiences, broken relationships, rejection, abandonment, unhealthy coping mechanisms. Also, years of emotional disappointment from one or both parents or an ex-partner(s). While time may pass, the underlying wounds often remain. Some people learn how to manage their pain, it becomes their identity but never truly heal from it.

Others attempt to find freedom through external solutions while neglecting the deeper issues of the heart. They may distance themselves from painful relationships, change environments, adopt new habits, or pursue various spiritual practices, like burning sage or other incense.

They believe these actions alone will bring separation from demonic presence and eventual peace. In fact, burning sage or incense can sometimes invite demons in. Yet true healing requires more than changing circumstances. It requires confronting the root causes of the pain, embracing truth, extending forgiveness where necessary, and allowing God to restore the broken places within through inner healing and spiritual deliverance. Jesus even said it in His ministry.

Many wounded and broken people carry emotional, spiritual, and psychological attachments from past relationships long after those relationships have ended. The person may be gone, but the pain and soul-tie remain. The memories remain. The rejection remains. The anger, fear, abandonment, and disappointment remain. These unresolved issues continue to influence future relationships in ways they often do not recognize.

The deception is believing that external actions alone can solve an internal problem.

You can block a phone number and still carry the wound.

You can move to another city and still carry the pain.

You can avoid the person and still remain emotionally connected to the trauma they created. And until it's broken, they remain connected through the soul-tie created from having sex together.

That also includes ungodly soul-ties with ex-spouses whom you had sex with prior to marriage.

The real issue is not always the relationship itself but what was left behind after it ended. The fragmented pieces which cause the spiritual nightmare that the demonic realm feeds off of.

Many people spend years trying to escape the symptoms while never addressing the root cause. They attempt to manage the hurt with Therapy rather than heal from it completely. As a result, the same patterns repeat themselves over and over again. Different faces enter their lives, but the same unhealed wounds continue to dictate their decisions. The results are always the same, another failed relationship. And it's always someone else's fault.

Healing begins when a person becomes willing to confront what happened, acknowledge the damage it caused, forgive where necessary, and allow God to restore the broken places within them through inner healing and spiritual deliverance.

Until then, the past continues to exert influence over the present.

One of the characteristics of a healed and whole person is their willingness to deal honestly with their past. A wounded and broken person often believes they have moved on simply because enough time has passed. But time alone does not heal wounds. Time only reveals whether healing has actually taken place.

As I sat there and listened to a conversation she and I were having, I couldn't help but see the connection between the unresolved pain and the defensive reactions. The little girl who had been hurt was still influencing the woman she had become.

The tragedy of woundedness is that many people believe surviving is the same thing as healing.

It isn't.

You can survive trauma and still be wounded.

You can function in life and still be broken.

You can attend church, serve in ministry, quote scripture, and still carry unresolved pain from decades ago.

Many people confuse coping with healing. They have learned how to manage the symptoms, but they have never addressed the root cause. The wound is simply hidden beneath layers of success, activity, religion, or self-confidence.

A healed and whole person does not fear examination because they understand that growth requires honesty. A wounded and broken person often fears examination because exposing the wound means confronting pain they have spent years trying to avoid.

One of the most difficult lessons I learned was that you cannot heal someone who refuses to acknowledge they are hurting.

No amount of love can do it.

No amount of patience can do it.

No amount of wisdom can do it.

Healing begins when a person becomes willing to admit that something is wrong.

The difference between being healed and whole and remaining wounded and broken is often found in a person's willingness to honestly examine their heart. Healing begins when denial ends. Freedom begins when truth is embraced.

As I reflect on that relationship now, I realize those conversations revealed far more than I understood at the time. They were not simply disagreements. They were indicators of unresolved wounds, buried pain, and issues that had never truly been addressed. The therapy she had only taught coping skills and not how to eliminate the issues all together for true absolute healing and wholeness.

The question is not whether we have been wounded. Every one of us has.

The question is whether we are willing to acknowledge those wounds and allow God to heal them when we're ready to take the necessary steps towards inner healing and spiritual deliverance.

That is the difference between being healed and whole or remaining wounded and broken.

That experience taught me something I will never forget: wounded people often crave love while simultaneously fearing it. They want to be seen, but they are terrified of exposure. They want intimacy, but they do not know how to live without self-protection, walls up. They want peace, but their inner world has been trained to expect disappointment. They want someone to stay, but they have already rehearsed abandonment in their minds so many times that trust feels dangerous.

And this is one of the greatest tragedies of brokenness. It does not only wound the person carrying it. It also reshapes the way they interpret true love when it finally arrives. Sometimes the greatest heartbreak is not that a person was never loved. It is that they were loved, but their wounds would not allow them to receive it fully and they sabotaged and rejected it unknowingly.

The more I reflected on my experiences, the more I began to see that this issue is bigger than dating. This is not just about romantic disappointment. This is about the condition of men, women and children everywhere. This is about the silent fractures carried from childhood into adulthood. This is about abandonment, betrayal, rejection, grief, trauma, neglect, fear, pride, insecurity, and pain that has gone unaddressed for years. This is about people building lives while internally bleeding. This is about how heart wounds, spiritual confusion, and unresolved pain affect not only relationships and marriages, but identity, decision-making, and purpose. And it affects the ability to walk in joy, peace and happiness by deceiving them in to believing they are.

That is why I felt compelled to write this book.

I did not write it merely to point out what is wrong in other people.

I wrote it because my eyes were opened.

I wrote it because I have seen how common, brokenness really is.

I wrote it because too many people are living under the illusion and deception that functioning is the same as healing.

It is not.

A person can work, smile, date, parent, worship, achieve, and still be deeply broken inside. A person can look fine on the surface and still be driven by fear, guarded by pain, and unable to sustain healthy love because they're living in denial.

My prayer is that this book will bring hidden things into the light. My hope is that it will help people recognize the wounds they have normalized, the patterns they have excused, and the pain they have buried.

I want it to challenge the person who believes they are fine simply because they have learned how to cope. I want it to reach the person who keeps sabotaging love, resisting truth, or repeating cycles they do not fully understand.

And I want it to encourage those who are tired of living in fragments, that healing is still possible.

Because no matter how widespread brokenness may be, it does not have to be the end of the story.

With 75% of the world being broken, one of the greatest needs of our time is not simply success, status, information, or even attraction.

Perhaps one of the greatest needs is healing.

Real healing. Deep healing.

The kind that reaches beneath behavior and gets to the root. The kind that restores what pain distorted.

The kind that makes a person whole from the inside out.

The kind God intended all along.

Therapy can be helpful in teaching a person how to understand their pain, regulate their emotions, and develop coping skills for the challenges they face.

But in most cases, it does not fully bring a person into complete healing and wholeness. It helps manage the symptoms of brokenness without reaching and resolving the deepest roots of the pain and removing the spiritual attachments that accompany it.

As a result, a person may function better, communicate better, and cope better, while still carrying unresolved issues beneath the surface that need complete healing.

This book was born out of heartbreak and revelation. It was born from seeing what I could no longer unsee. It was born from realizing that brokenness is everywhere, and that too many people are trying to build love, relationships and even marriage on foundations that have never truly been repaired.

It was born from a desire to expose what is hidden, name what is real, and point people toward a path of healing and wholeness.

So before we go any further, let this serve as both a confession and an invitation.

My confession is this: I once thought I was just having bad experiences in relationships, when in reality I was being confronted by a much larger truth about human brokenness.

And my invitation is this: as you read these pages, be honest enough to ask yourself where brokenness may still be speaking in your own life. Do you exhibit any or all of the characteristics you're about to read?

Because healing does not begin when we blame others. Healing begins when we are willing to see clearly, accept the truth and stop living in denial and take responsibility for our actions.

And sometimes, my friend, that is the very first act of mercy.

Chapter 1
What Is Brokenness?

Brokenness is one of the most misunderstood realities affecting humanity.

Most people assume brokenness only exists when someone's life is visibly collapsing. They imagine addiction, emotional breakdowns, homelessness, violence, or obvious instability. They picture people whose pain is easy to recognize from the outside.

But some of the most broken people in the world appear completely functional.

Some are wealthy.
Some are educated.
Some are successful.
Some are married.
Some sit faithfully in church every Sunday.
Some own businesses.
Some preach sermons.
Some lead ministries.
Some raise families.
Some smile publicly while privately battling torment they cannot explain.
They are also, some of the most beautiful people in the world.

Brokenness is dangerous precisely because it often hides itself behind functionality.

A person can be deeply broken and still appear disciplined.

They can still work.
Still provide.
Still lead.
Still inspire others.
Still quote scripture.
Still look confident.
Still appear emotionally composed.

But underneath the image there are fractures.

Fractures in identity.
Fractures in emotions.
Fractures in thinking.
Fractures in relationships.
Fractures in the soul.

Brokenness begins when wounds remain unresolved long enough to shape the way a person thinks, reacts, loves, trusts, handles conflict, receives correction, and sees themselves.

Some people were wounded through rejection.
Others through abandonment.
Others through betrayal.
Fatherless daughters or sons.
Abuse.
Neglect.
Humiliation.
Constant criticism.
Sexual trauma.
Fear.
Loss.
Shame.

Others became broken through persistent sinful choices.

Fornication.
Pride.
Lust.
Bitterness.
Hatred.
Manipulation.
Unforgiveness.
Greed.
Addiction.
Rebellion.

Sometimes brokenness comes through what happened to a person.

Sometimes it comes through what a person continually allows within themselves.

Either way, unresolved brokenness eventually begins controlling behavior.

The frightening part is that many people do not heal from brokenness. They simply learn how to manage it.

This is one reason many remain trapped for decades.

Modern culture has become very skilled at teaching coping mechanisms, through traditional therapy, while rarely confronting the spiritual roots. People are often taught how to temporarily calm anxiety, manage emotional reactions, regulate behavior, or function through pain without ever truly becoming whole.

Even therapy, while sometimes helpful for identifying trauma, patterns, emotional wounds, or destructive thinking, often only teaches people how to manage brokenness rather than truly heal it.

A person may learn:
- Breathing techniques
- Emotional regulation
- Communication skills
- Boundary setting
- Behavioral awareness

Yet still remain deeply wounded internally.

Why?

Because management or coping is not transformation.

A person can intellectually understand their trauma while still being spiritually bound by fear, pride, rage, lust, rejection, shame, or unforgiveness.

They can explain their wounds while still living from them.

They can describe their dysfunction while remaining controlled by it.

Many people become educated about their brokenness without ever becoming free from it.

They become highly self-aware prisoners.

They know why they react the way they do.
Why they fear intimacy.
Why they sabotage relationships.
Why they become defensive.
Why they shut down emotionally.

But understanding pain is not the same as healing from it.

A person can spend years discussing childhood wounds while never surrendering the pride, bitterness, fear, or spiritual strongholds attached to those wounds.

This is why some people remain in cycles despite years of counseling, conversations, books, seminars, or emotional breakthroughs.

The root was never removed.

Because true healing is not merely psychological.

It is spiritual.

Brokenness is not only emotional damage. It grants demonic access through the brokenness.

Many people have wounds that became open doors.

Doors for torment.
Doors for deception.
Doors for rage.
Doors for addiction.
Doors for fear.
Doors for pride.
Doors for hatred.
Doors for sexual perversion.
Doors for self-destruction.

The enemy thrives in unresolved places of brokenness.

Not every struggle is demonic.

But unresolved wounds often become territories where lies gain strength.

A rejected person begins believing:
"I am unwanted."

An abandoned person believes:
"People always leave."

A wounded man believes:
"Vulnerability is weakness."

A betrayed woman believes:
"Control is the only way to stay safe."

Over time these lies become internal agreements.

And agreements with lies create spiritual strongholds.

That stronghold then begins influencing behavior, relationships, emotional reactions, and even spiritual deception.

This is why brokenness often survives beneath outward success.

Some people build entire lives around protecting wounds instead of healing them.

Some become emotionally detached because closeness feels dangerous.
Some become controlling because chaos once wounded them deeply.
Some become hyper-independent because trusting people led to disappointment.
Some become prideful because vulnerability feels humiliating.
Some become addicted to validation because rejection hollowed them out internally.

Eventually survival mechanisms stop feeling temporary.

They begin feeling normal.

The person no longer says:
"I developed this because I was wounded."

Now they say:
"This is just who I am."

That sentence has imprisoned countless people because now it's their identity.

Because once dysfunction becomes identity, healing begins feeling threatening.

Why?

Because healing would require the person to confront the very thing they built their personality around.

Brokenness hides itself behind masks.

One of the greatest masks is pride.

Pride is not always loud arrogance.

Sometimes pride looks like:
- Defensiveness
- Inability to apologize
- Emotional distance
- Refusing accountability
- Blaming others constantly
- Rejecting correction
- Hiding weakness
- Needing control
- Avoiding vulnerability
- Pretending to have no struggles

Pride protects wounds from exposure.

It convinces people to preserve appearances instead of pursuing freedom.

Many broken people become performers.

Performing peace.
Performing confidence.
Performing spirituality.
Performing strength.
Performing happiness.

But performance cannot heal the soul.

Some people know scripture yet remain emotionally unstable.
Some pray publicly while secretly consumed with rage privately.
Some preach forgiveness while feeding bitterness for years.
Some appear spiritually mature while remaining emotionally immature.

Brokenness creates contradiction.

The mouth says one thing while the soul lives another.

This is why activity should never be mistaken for healing.

A man can provide financially while remaining emotionally unavailable.
A woman can appear nurturing while manipulating everyone around her.
A leader can appear strong while secretly controlled by insecurity and fear of rejection.

Brokenness often hides itself inside functionality.

And because the person is still productive, they convince themselves they are healthy.

But fruit eventually exposes the type of tree it really is.

Broken people often wound others without realizing it.

The rejected reject others first.
The abandoned struggle trusting anyone.
The controlling create emotional exhaustion.
The prideful make honesty unsafe.
The angry spread instability into every environment they enter.

Unhealed wounds eventually become weapons.

And many people bleed on individuals who never cut them.

This is why true healing requires more than coping skills.

It requires transformation.

Not image management.
Not emotional suppression.
Not temporary behavior modification.
Transformation.

Healing requires:
- Truth
- Humility
- Repentance
- Accountability
- Deliverance
- Renewing the mind
- Confronting lies
- Surrendering pride
- Healing emotional wounds
- Restoring identity through God

Real healing reaches the roots.

It tears down false identities.
Exposes hidden wounds.
Breaks spiritual agreements with lies.
Confronts sin honestly.

Restores truth where deception once ruled.

But none of that can happen until a person first acknowledges they are broken.

And for many people, that is the hardest step of all.

Because functioning has convinced them they are free.

But surviving is not healing.

Managing pain is not wholeness.

And appearing strong is not the same as being delivered.

Chapter 2

The Masks People Wear

Broken people rarely reveal themselves immediately.

Most wounded individuals learn very early how to survive by hiding.

Some hide behind success.
Some behind religion.
Some behind attractiveness.
Some behind humor.
Some behind anger.
Some behind intelligence.
Some behind control.
Some behind silence.

The mask becomes protection.

What began as survival eventually becomes identity.

Many people no longer know where the mask ends and the real person begins.

The frightening reality is that some people wear masks for so long they eventually believe the performance themselves.

The successful businessman who secretly feels worthless.
The woman who appears strong but is terrified of vulnerability.
The church leader addicted to admiration.
The man who presents himself as emotionless because emotions feel unsafe.
The constantly joking person hiding depression.
The hyper-spiritual person using religion to avoid confronting emotional wounds.

Masks are rarely random.

They are usually built around pain.

And some of the deepest pain people carry comes from fractured relationships with parents.

A child's understanding of love, safety, affirmation, identity, emotional security, discipline, tenderness, and belonging is often shaped first through father and mother relationships.

When those bonds are broken, absent, cold, inconsistent, manipulative, abusive, or emotionally disconnected, the wounds often continue speaking long into adulthood.

An absentee father leaves deep fractures in both daughters and sons.

Many women carrying father wounds spend years searching externally for what was never established internally.

Some silently ask:
"Why wasn't I worth staying for?"

Even when never spoken aloud, the wound often remains beneath the surface.

For some women, this creates insecurity.
For others, fear of abandonment.
For others, emotional dependency.
For others, unhealthy attachment patterns.
For others, attraction to emotionally unavailable men because dysfunction feels familiar.

Some women become hyper-independent because depending on anyone feels unsafe.

Others use sexuality to seek affirmation they never received emotionally.

Others tolerate unhealthy relationships because rejection feels more familiar than healthy love.

Some women appear strong externally while internally battling the fear that they are unwanted, unseen, or replaceable.

The wound may not always appear obvious.

But it often reveals itself in relationship choices, emotional reactions, fear of vulnerability, trust issues, jealousy, insecurity, or the constant need for reassurance.

An absentee father also deeply affects sons.

Many boys grow up without guidance into manhood.

No affirmation.
No emotional presence.
No healthy example of masculinity.
No instruction.
No consistent discipline.
No model of strength balanced with love.

As a result, many men spend years trying to discover what manhood actually is.

Some become angry because abandonment created rage they never processed.

Some become emotionally detached because vulnerability was never modeled safely.

Some become hyper-aggressive because aggression feels stronger than weakness.

Some become passive because they never learned confidence.

Some seek identity through money, women, status, sex, achievement, or power because internally they still feel unseen.

Others become obsessed with proving themselves.

Proving they matter.
Proving they are enough.
Proving they are strong.
Proving they are successful.

Many men are not driven solely by ambition.

They are driven by unresolved wounds.

A father's absence often leaves a son searching for identity in places that can never truly satisfy him.

But father wounds are not the only wounds shaping brokenness.

A mother who fails to emotionally bond with her children can create equally devastating fractures.

A mother's nurture often shapes emotional safety, tenderness, connection, comfort, affection, emotional regulation, and the child's understanding of being emotionally valued.

When that bond is missing, distorted, manipulative, cold, inconsistent, critical, or emotionally absent, the effects often follow children into adulthood.

A daughter who never bonded emotionally with her mother may grow up struggling deeply with identity and emotional security.

Some women secretly feel impossible to love because the very person who was supposed to nurture them emotionally remained distant, critical, unavailable, jealous, harsh, or emotionally disconnected.

Some daughters grow up constantly chasing approval.

Others become emotionally guarded because vulnerability feels unsafe.

Some become highly sensitive to rejection.
Others become controlling.
Others become perfectionists trying to earn affection through performance.

Some women struggle to form healthy female relationships because competition, criticism, or emotional coldness shaped their understanding of womanhood itself.

Others become emotionally needy while simultaneously fearing intimacy.

Some become mothers themselves while secretly carrying wounds they never healed from their own mothers.

The pain often becomes generational.

A son affected by a disconnected mother may experience different but equally damaging fractures.

Many men who lacked maternal bonding struggle with emotional connection later in life.

Some grow up emotionally starved but unable to explain why.

A mother's warmth often teaches a son emotional safety.

When that warmth is absent, withheld, manipulative, overly critical, or inconsistent, some boys learn to disconnect emotionally from themselves entirely.

Some men later struggle expressing affection.
Some fear vulnerability deeply.
Some crave female validation compulsively.
Some become emotionally avoidant.
Some become addicted to lust because sexual pursuit feels easier than emotional intimacy.

Others become angry because underneath the anger is emotional deprivation they never processed honestly.

Some men spend their lives searching for nurturing through relationships, sex, achievement, or attention because something foundational remained empty internally.

Broken children often become adults still trying to satisfy childhood wounds.

And many do not realize their adult behaviors are still being driven by unresolved pain from decades earlier.

This is how cycles survive.

The absent father creates the wounded son.
The wounded son becomes the emotionally unavailable husband.
The emotionally unavailable husband later becomes the disconnected father.

An emotionally disconnected mother often wounds her daughter in ways that are not immediately visible.
The wounded daughter grows up emotionally guarded, carrying walls she built to protect herself.
Later, as a wife, she may struggle to fully engage emotionally in her marriage. Then, as a mother, she may struggle to bond deeply with her own children because she never experienced healthy emotional connection herself. What is not healed is often repeated from one generation to the next.

Brokenness reproduces itself when wounds remain unhealed.

This is why masks become so dangerous.

Masks do not solve wounds.

They only conceal them.

The wounded man hides behind anger.
The wounded woman hides behind control.
The insecure hide behind pride.
The fearful hide behind isolation.
The rejected hide behind performance.
The ashamed hide behind image management.

Brokenness often disguises itself as strength.

But many people are not operating from strength.

They are operating from protection.

There is a difference.

A healed person can be open without collapsing emotionally.

A broken person often feels unsafe without walls.

This is why intimacy becomes terrifying for many wounded individuals.

Intimacy threatens masks.

To truly know someone requires exposure.

And exposure terrifies people who spent their lives surviving through protection.

Many secretly fear:
- Rejection
- Abandonment
- Shame
- Weakness
- Vulnerability
- Being truly seen
- Losing control

So instead of healing, they adapt.

They create safer versions of themselves.

Some become performers.

They know how to sound spiritually mature.
Emotionally stable.
Wise.
Confident.
Peaceful.

But performance is not transformation.

Many people know how to imitate healing without ever experiencing healing.

Religion is one of the most common masks wounded people use.

Not genuine intimacy with God.

Religious performance.

Some use church activity, scripture knowledge, ministry involvement, or spiritual language to avoid confronting unresolved emotional wounds within themselves.

They learn how to appear spiritually mature while remaining emotionally fractured.
They pray publicly while battling rage privately.
They preach forgiveness while secretly feeding bitterness.
They worship passionately while remaining trapped in pride, lust, manipulation, fear, or control.

The mask of spirituality becomes dangerous because it convinces both the individual and others that transformation has already occurred.

But activity is not freedom.

Noise is not healing.

Emotion is not deliverance.

Some people cry during worship services yet remain unchanged because tears alone do not heal what pride still protects.

One of the most damaging masks is silence.

Some people use silence to punish others emotionally while appearing calm externally.

The man who withdraws emotionally after conflict often believes silence protects him from vulnerability.

But silence can become manipulation.

Instead of communicating honestly, he retreats emotionally, forcing others to carry the tension while he maintains control through distance.

To outsiders he may appear peaceful.

But emotional shutdown is not peace.

Some masks are loud.

Others are quiet.

Both can hide brokenness equally well.

Humor is another common mask.

Some people joke constantly because silence would force them to confront pain they have spent years avoiding.

Busyness can become a mask too.

Many people stay constantly occupied because stillness exposes what movement hides.

They work nonstop.
Build nonstop.
Serve nonstop.
Move nonstop.

But underneath the activity there is unrest. Their mind is constantly racing. Often times they have sleep issues.

Some people are not driven by purpose.

They are driven by avoidance.

Brokenness constantly searches for protection apart from healing.

And masks create temporary safety.

But temporary safety eventually becomes long-term bondage.

Because masks prevent honesty.

And honesty is necessary for healing.

Truth threatens the identity people carefully constructed.

Correction feels offensive.
Accountability feels unsafe.
Transparency feels dangerous.

Why?

Because masks survive through protection.

But healing requires exposure.

This is why deliverance becomes difficult for many people.

Not because God is unwilling to free them.

But because brokenness often convinces people to protect the very thing destroying them.

The enemy thrives in hidden places.

Darkness survives through concealment.

Pride says:
"Hide it."

Fear says:
"Protect yourself."

Shame says:
"If people truly knew you, they would reject you."

But freedom begins when a person becomes tired of performing.

Healing begins when masks fall.

Because masks may protect wounds temporarily.

But they can never heal them.

Chapter 3

The Fatherless Daughter – The Wound That Echoes Through A Lifetime

"A father to the fatherless, a defender of widows, is God in His holy dwelling." — Psalm 68:5

When people hear the phrase **fatherless daughter**, they often picture a little girl whose father died or abandoned the family.

Sometimes that is true.

But fatherlessness is much deeper than physical absence.

Many women grew up in homes where their father came home every night, paid the bills, attended school functions, and lived under the same roof—but emotionally, he was unavailable.

He never affirmed.
He never protected.
He never nurtured.
He never listened.
He never embraced.
He never truly knew his daughter.

A father can be physically present while emotionally absent.

In many ways, emotional abandonment leaves wounds just as deep as physical abandonment because the child constantly asks herself:

"Why doesn't my own father choose me?"

A healthy father provides more than food and shelter.

He helps shape a daughter's identity.

He teaches her what love looks like.

He demonstrates how a woman should be treated.

He becomes her first example of masculine strength, protection, affection, discipline, consistency, and security.

His approval tells her:

"You matter."

"You're beautiful."

"You're valuable."

"You deserve respect."

Without realizing it, fathers help answer questions daughters never ask aloud.

Am I enough?

Am I lovable?

Am I worth protecting?

Am I worth pursuing?

When those questions remain unanswered, many girls spend decades trying to answer those themselves.

Many fatherless girls develop survival behaviors long before they understand why.

Some become overly independent.

Others become people pleasers.

Some become perfectionists.

Others quietly withdraw.

Others become promiscuous.

Many become the "good girl," hoping achievement will finally earn the attention they never received.

Others become rebellious because negative attention feels better than no attention at all.

Some stop believing men can be trusted before they are old enough to understand what trust even means.

The wound begins forming long before adulthood.

One of the deepest longings inside many fatherless daughters is validation.

Every little girl wants her father to notice her.

She wants him to smile when she enters the room.

She wants him to tell her she's beautiful.

She wants to feel safe in his presence.

When that never happens, many women unknowingly spend years searching for someone else to provide what was never received at home.

This does not make them weak.

It makes them wounded.

Some seek validation through relationships.

Others through achievement.

Others through appearance.

Others through sexuality.

Others through social media.

Others through careers.

Others through ministry.

Validation becomes addictive because the wound underneath remains unresolved.

Many fatherless daughters were never taught the difference between attention and genuine love.

Attention feels exciting.

Love feels safe.

Attention pursues.

Love protects.

Attention wants something.

Love gives something.

Attention is temporary.

Love is committed.

Without a healthy father modeling these differences, some women accept unhealthy relationships simply because someone finally noticed them.

Predators often recognize this before the woman does.

They know how to offer temporary affirmation while secretly pursuing control.

What begins as feeling "chosen" often ends in manipulation.

One common result of father wounds is an overwhelming fear of rejection.

Rejection becomes more than disappointment.

It becomes confirmation.

Every breakup feels like childhood repeating itself.

Every criticism sounds like abandonment.

Every unanswered text feels personal.

Every disagreement feels like someone preparing to leave.

The emotional reaction often has less to do with the present relationship than the unresolved wound from the past.

Many fatherless daughters live expecting people to leave.

Sometimes they cling too tightly.

Sometimes they push people away first.

Sometimes they sabotage healthy relationships before they become serious.

It feels safer to leave than to be left.

They convince themselves:

"If I never fully trust anyone, I can never be abandoned again."

Unfortunately, the walls that protect them from pain also prevent intimacy.

Trust is learned.

Children learn trust by watching consistency.

Promises kept.

Protection provided.

Affection demonstrated.

Presence maintained.

When a father repeatedly disappoints, disappears, lies, abuses, or neglects his daughter, trust becomes dangerous.

As adults, many women desperately desire healthy love while simultaneously fearing it.

The conflict is exhausting.

Many fatherless daughters quietly decide:

"I will never need anyone."

What appears to be strength is often self-protection.

They become highly successful.

Highly capable.

Highly responsible.

Highly independent.

Yet privately exhausted.

They struggle receiving help.

They struggle depending on others.

They struggle allowing themselves to be cared for.

The wound whispers:

"People always leave. Depend on yourself."

People often choose what feels familiar rather than what is healthy.

A daughter raised around emotional distance often feels strangely comfortable with emotionally unavailable men.

Chaos feels normal.

Inconsistency feels familiar.

Distance feels expected.

Healthy men sometimes feel boring because peace feels unfamiliar.

Brokenness often reproduces itself until someone intentionally interrupts the cycle.

A father's affirmation plays a powerful role in shaping identity.

Without it, many daughters spend years asking:

Who am I?

Am I enough?

Why wasn't I worth staying for?

Was something wrong with me?

Children rarely blame absent parents.

They blame themselves.

The child assumes:

"If Dad left, something must be wrong with me."

That lie can quietly influence decisions for decades.

Some fatherless daughters appear incredibly strong.

Successful.

Confident.

Independent.

Resilient.

Yet underneath lives unresolved grief.

Sometimes anger.

Sometimes disappointment.

Sometimes deep sadness.

The little girl inside never stopped hoping Dad would finally show up emotionally.

Many women spend adulthood pretending they no longer care.

But pretending is not healing.

Father wounds often surface after marriage.

Some women struggle receiving healthy leadership because authority feels unsafe.

Others become overly controlling because control feels protective.

Some constantly test their husbands.

Others expect abandonment.

Some become emotionally guarded.

Others become overly dependent.

None of these reactions necessarily reflect a lack of love.

They often reflect unresolved fear.

Many women become exceptional mothers precisely because they refuse to repeat what they experienced.

Others become emotionally overwhelmed because parenting awakens childhood memories they thought had disappeared.

Watching a loving father interact with his daughter can unexpectedly trigger grief.

Not because it is wrong.

Because it reveals what was missing.

Healing often begins when hidden grief is finally acknowledged.

The goal is not to spend life blaming fathers.

Some fathers were wounded themselves.

Some repeated what they experienced.

Some never learned healthy fatherhood.

Others genuinely tried but failed.

Understanding someone's brokenness does not excuse the damage.

But forgiveness allows healing to begin.

Healing is not pretending the wound never existed.

Healing is refusing to allow the wound to determine the rest of your life.

No father can perfectly provide everything a daughter needs.

Every human father eventually falls short.

But unresolved father wounds do not have to become a lifelong prison.

Healing begins with honesty.

Honesty about what happened.

Honesty about what was missing.

Honesty about how those experiences shaped beliefs, relationships, fears, and expectations.

Awareness is not weakness.

It is the beginning of freedom.

The little girl who longed to be chosen can become the woman who no longer bases her worth on someone else's approval.

The daughter who feared abandonment can learn secure attachment.

The woman who confused attention with love can learn the difference.

The cycle can end.

What was broken can be healed.

And what is healed no longer has to be repeated.

Chapter 4
Men Raised By The Streets

The men who grow up without a father in their lives, or with one who never truly taught them anything, often carry a kind of ache they do not always know how to name. It does not always show up as sadness.

More often, it appears as anger, emotional distance, pride, impulsiveness, confusion, or a constant need to prove something.

From the outside, some of these men look strong, independent, and self-made. But underneath that image is often a boy who had to piece together manhood from fragments, guesswork, and survival.

A father is meant to do more than simply exist in the home. He is supposed to help form a son's inner world.

He teaches him:
how to think through life.
how to carry responsibility.
how to respond to pressure.
how to treat women.
how to handle conflict.
how to work.
how to lead.
how to remain steady when emotions rise.

He helps a boy develop identity before the world starts shaping one for him.

Without that kind of guidance, a young man is often left searching for direction in places that were never designed to raise him.

When a father is absent, silent, detached, or unequipped, something else usually fills the gap. For many men, the streets become the teacher. Peer culture becomes the standard.

In today's world, social media becomes the mentor. Music, entertainment, and online personalities begin feeding them a version of manhood that is often built on image rather than substance.

Little by little, they start learning lessons from people who are wounded themselves.

So they are told that being a man means hiding emotion, avoiding vulnerability, dominating others, collecting women, chasing money, and making sure nobody ever sees their weakness.

They learn that anger looks stronger than tenderness, detachment feels safer than trust, and control seems more dependable than love. No one stops to explain that these are often survival responses, not signs of maturity.

No one teaches them that hardness is not the same thing as strength.

Many of these men become experts at surviving, but they never truly learn how to be whole or how to love.

They learn how to perform confidence without ever developing peace.

They learn how to keep moving without ever healing.

They learn how to protect themselves without knowing how to connect.

They learn how to talk like leaders without ever being led through the deeper work of character and developing integrity.

That is one of the quiet tragedies of fatherlessness.

A boy may grow older, stronger, and more experienced, but still remain emotionally underdeveloped because nobody showed him what healthy manhood looked like.

He may know:
how to hustle.
how to attract attention.
how to fight.
how to earn.

But he may not know:
how to listen.
how to apologize.
how to stay.
how to lead with gentleness.
how to carry love without fear.
how to be vulnerable.
how to be transparent.
How to be humble.

Social media has intensified this problem. It gives many men quick access to information, but not necessarily wisdom.

It teaches:

- branding before identity
- performance before substance
- reaction before reflection

A man can scroll through thousands of opinions about masculinity, relationships, money, and power, yet still remain deeply lost inside.

He may learn how to sound insightful without ever becoming grounded. He may speak with certainty while quietly carrying confusion.

The danger is that repeated exposure to wounded voices can normalize wounded living. Men begin imitating what gets attention instead of what produces stability.

They mistake popularity for truth and noise for authority.

They absorb bitterness and call it discernment.
They absorb emotional numbness and call it discipline.
They absorb distrust and call it wisdom.

Over time, the false version of manhood begins to feel natural simply because they have seen it so often.

What many people do not realize is that men raised this way are often compensating for something much deeper. The man who constantly needs control may be covering insecurity.

The man who keeps multiple women in his life may be reaching for validation.

The man who never opens up may be protecting old heart wounds he never had language for.

The man who shuts down under pressure may never have learned how to process disappointment, fear, or correction in a healthy way.

The man who seems arrogant may be deeply unfamiliar with peace.

Sometimes the absence of a father does not just create a knowledge gap; it creates an identity heart wound.

A son is left asking questions he may never say out loud:

- What does it mean to be a man?
- Am I enough?

- Why was I not worth staying for?
- Who am I supposed to become?
- How do I lead when nobody led me?
- How do I build what was never modeled for me?

Those questions do not disappear just because a man gets older. They often remain underneath the surface, shaping relationships, choices, fears, and habits for years.

This is why some men become emotionally unavailable, chronically defensive, commitment-avoidant, hyper-independent, or allergic to correction.

It is not always because they are heartless. Sometimes it is because nobody ever taught them how to feel safe in honesty.

Nobody taught them how to receive love without suspicion, or accountability without shame.

Nobody taught them that strength can coexist with softness, or that maturity includes humility.

The wounds of fatherlessness often spill into every area of life.

A man may struggle in relationships because he does not know how to stay present.

He may struggle in marriage because he confuses authority with control.

He may struggle with work because discipline was never formed.

He may struggle with purpose because deep inside he still feels unanchored.

He may become a father himself while secretly carrying grief over the kind of father he never had.

And if that pain remains unaddressed, it can quietly shape his entire life.

He may build his identity around compensation.
He may chase money to silence shame.
He may chase women to quiet rejection.
He may chase respect because he never felt seen.
He may keep proving himself, performing, achieving, and striving, all while never slowing down long enough to admit that a part of him is still hurting.

Yet there is another way forward.

Healing begins when a man becomes honest about what was missing and how deeply it affected him.

It begins when he stops romanticizing survival and starts acknowledging the cost of it.

It begins when he realizes that coping is not the same as healing, and performance is not the same as peace.

It begins when he allows himself to grieve what he did not receive instead of pretending he never needed it.

That grieving matters.

A man cannot become whole by mocking his own pain or burying it beneath ambition, lust, entertainment, or distraction.

He has to face it.
He has to name the abandonment, the silence, the lack of guidance, the confusion, the anger, and the ache.

He has to admit that being forced to raise himself left scars.

He has to be willing to unlearn what broken environments taught him and to rebuild from a healthier foundation.

That rebuilding usually requires more than information. It requires wise voices, healing relationships, honest self-examination, and a willingness to be taught.

It may come through mentorship, counseling, mature friendships, restorative community, disciplined reflection, and the quiet work of learning a better way to live.

Over time, a man can begin to replace:

- Reaction with reflection
- Control with steadiness
- Image with integrity

He can learn that real strength is not emotional shutdown.

Real strength is the ability to remain grounded, truthful, and responsible even when life is painful.

Real leadership is not domination; it is stewardship.

Real maturity is not pretending to have all the answers; it is being teachable enough to grow.

Real confidence is not loud or performative; it is settled. It does not need constant applause because it is rooted more deeply.

There is also a deeper hope available to men who were not fathered well. Even when human guidance was missing, their story does not have to end in emptiness, confusion, or repetition.

There is still a higher pattern of wisdom, truth, and restoration that can re-form what life left unfinished.

A man can be rebuilt:
He can be softened without becoming weak.
He can be disciplined without becoming harsh.
He can become trustworthy, steady, loving, and clear-minded even if he did not grow up seeing those qualities modeled around him.

That process takes:

1. Humility.
2. Time.
3. Courage to admit that what looked like strength was sometimes defense, and what looked like independence was sometimes isolation.
4. Courage to let go of false lessons and receive better ones.

But this is where real change begins.

- A man who was never properly taught can still learn.
- A man who was not guided can still be led.
- A man who was raised by wounded systems can still be healed enough to stop repeating them.
- A man who was abandoned can still become dependable.
- A man who never felt affirmed can still develop a grounded sense of identity.
- A man who never saw healthy love can still learn how to give it.

And perhaps one of the most beautiful forms of restoration is this:

A man who grew up without wise fathering can, through healing, humility, and truth, become the very kind of man he once needed.

Can become:
Steady where life was unstable.
Present where others were absent.
Gentle where others were hard.
Clear where so much around him was confused.

In that sense, his healing does not only change him. It changes what he passes forward and those around him.

Chapter 5

The Woman Who Waited Too Long

There is a unique silence that surrounds some women after the age of forty-five.

It is not the silence of peace.
It is not the silence of contentment.

It is the silence that settles in after years of distractions, independence, relationships that went nowhere, guarded hearts, career pursuits, hidden disappointments, and private questions that never received honest answers.

Some women reach this stage of life never having been married and never having had children.

On the outside, many appear strong, successful, polished, intelligent, spiritual, accomplished, and emotionally stable. They have learned how to survive alone. Some have built careers, businesses, ministries, social circles, or lifestyles that keep them busy enough to avoid confronting the deeper ache within them.

But late at night, when the noise fades, many wrestle with questions they never imagined they would still be asking.

"What happened?"

"How did I get here?"

"Why did nothing ever work out?"

"Was it them… or was it me?"

The world teaches women that time is always on their side. It teaches them they can postpone love, marriage, family, healing, submission, softness, and emotional growth indefinitely.

Society tells them they lose nothing by waiting.

In fact, modern culture often says to woman "you don't need a man." Yet God said it is not good for man to be alone, I'll make him a helpmate.

But time is one thing no human being defeats.

A woman can delay many things in life, but eventually reality arrives.

The body changes. Fertility changes. Energy changes. Desires change. Priorities change. And eventually, loneliness begins speaking louder than pride ever did.

For some women, singleness after forty-five is not a tragedy. Some truly have peace, purpose, emotional health, and a genuine calling to live differently. But for many others, the issue is not singleness itself.

The issue is unresolved brokenness.

Because there are women who deeply desire love, marriage, intimacy, companionship, and family, yet unknowingly sabotage every opportunity that comes near them.

Some do not realize that years of unhealed pain can slowly begin to reshape a woman's identity.

What started as heart wounds from rejection, abandonment, disappointment, or betrayal can, over time, harden the heart and affect the way she sees herself, others, and even God.

She may begin to come across as selfish, guarded, harsh, or ornery, but often those behaviors are rooted in deeper pain, unresolved hurt, and spiritual brokenness rather than simply her true nature.

When those wounds are left unhealed, the enemy can use them to distort her personality, strengthen unhealthy patterns, and keep her from walking in the softness, freedom, and wholeness God intended for her.

A woman who was disappointed enough times may stop trusting men altogether.

A woman abandoned emotionally by her father may struggle to bond deeply with masculine leadership.

A woman who watched unhealthy relationships growing up may normalize dysfunction while rejecting healthy love because it feels unfamiliar.

A woman who was betrayed, abused, rejected, cheated on, neglected, or emotionally wounded may eventually build walls so high that even good men cannot reach her.

Over time, independence becomes armor.

Control becomes safety.

Distance becomes protection.

And eventually, what once protected her begins isolating her.

Many women over forty-five who have never married have become extremely skilled at self-preservation.

They know how to avoid vulnerability.
They know how to remain emotionally guarded while appearing emotionally available.
They know how to maintain companionship without true surrender.
They know how to keep a man interested while simultaneously keeping him at arm's length.

Often, they do not even realize they are doing it.

Some have spent decades blaming “the wrong men” while never confronting the patterns within themselves.

Others became addicted to unrealistic expectations. They built fantasy versions of relationships that no real man could fulfill.

Every man was compared against an invisible checklist shaped by pain, social media, pride, fear, trauma, or unresolved disappointment.

Then years passed.

And another year passed.

And another.

Until eventually the dating pool changed.

The attention changed.

The opportunities changed.

And suddenly the woman who once believed she had endless options realizes life does not pause for anyone.

One of the greatest deceptions in modern culture is convincing women that healing is unnecessary as long as they remain functional.

Many women have attended therapy.
Many have learned coping skills.
Many can articulate their emotions extremely well.
Many can explain trauma intellectually.

But intellectual awareness is not true healing.

A person can understand their wounds while still being controlled by them.

A person can recognize unhealthy patterns while still repeating them.

A person can attend counseling for years and still remain emotionally unavailable, bitter, fearful, defensive, prideful, masculine in spirit, or incapable of healthy intimacy.

And spiritually, many people never consider that their battles are deeper than psychology alone. That at the center of everything, it's spiritual.

The enemy thrives in hidden heart wounds. That's his job description and it's like an addictive drug to him and his army, it's where they gain momentum.

Childhood rejection.
Abandonment.
Trauma.
Sexual abuse or assault.
Rape.
Fear.
Bitterness.
Unforgiveness.
Soul ties.
Toxic agreements.
Deep disappointment.
Self-hatred.
Fear of men.
Fear of submission.
Fear of vulnerability.

These open doors spiritually, emotionally, and mentally.

The demonic realm doesn't announce itself. They slide in quietly through the open doors from the heart wounds and trauma(s).

They're behind the personality traits people normalize, residing in the shadows of your life.

Isolation.
Control.
Pride.
Fear of intimacy.
Chronic distrust.
Emotional instability.
Constant confusion.
Self-sabotage.
Bitterness disguised as strength.

And because many women become highly functional, successful, attractive, educated, or spiritual on the surface, no one ever challenges what is happening underneath.

Instead, culture celebrates it.

A wounded woman is often told:
"Protect your peace."
"Stay guarded."
"Never submit."
"Men are intimidated by strong women."
"Love yourself first."
"Keep your options open."

But eventually many women discover that endless self-protection also prevents genuine connection.

A relationship cannot thrive where vulnerability never exists.

A healthy man eventually grows exhausted trying to love a woman who constantly anticipates betrayal.

Some women over forty-five are still carrying unresolved pain from men who hurt them twenty years earlier. Others are still reacting emotionally to fathers who failed them in childhood. Some are still trying to prove their worth through accomplishments because they never truly felt chosen, seen, protected, or loved.

The tragedy is not simply aging alone.
The tragedy is never becoming whole.

Because healing changes everything.

A healed woman does not need manipulation to feel secure.
A healed woman does not weaponize:

- Silence
- Control
- Sex
- Independence
- Emotional withdrawal

A healed woman can receive love without suspicion.

Then:
She can communicate honestly.
She can apologize.
She can trust wisely without becoming paranoid.
She can embrace femininity without seeing it as weakness.
She can respect masculine leadership without feeling inferior.
She can discern healthy men instead of constantly chasing unhealthy excitement.
She can express gratitude.

Most importantly, a healed woman stops blaming everyone else for the outcomes of her life.

There are also women who sacrificed their opportunity for marriage because they continually prioritized temporary pleasure, casual relationships, career ambition, pride, unrealistic standards, or emotional unavailability over building something lasting.

Modern society rarely warns women that seasons matter.

There is:
A season for building.
A season for marriage.
A season for children.
A season for family.

And while grace exists, time still moves forward.

Many women assumed they could always revisit those desires later.

Until later arrived.

Then suddenly they found themselves sitting in beautiful homes filled with silence.

Successful careers that feel empty at night.

Social media accounts full of smiling pictures hiding private loneliness.

Trips. Brunches. Events. Girls nights. Luxury purchases. Filters. Motivational quotes.

Yet internally wondering why peace still feels absent. Or even worse, being deceived in to thinking they're at peace.

The human heart was never designed to be fulfilled by appearances alone.

And many women eventually realize that independence without intimacy can become its own prison.

Still, this chapter is not written to condemn those women.

It is written to confront reality with honesty.

Because there is still hope wherever humility exists.

Some women over forty-five finally begin healing for real. Not surface healing. Not image management. Not motivational slogans. Real healing.

The kind where they finally confront the pain they spent decades avoiding.

The kind where they forgive.

The kind where they stop pretending.

The kind where they allow God to expose the broken places hidden beneath the polished exterior.

The kind where pride dies.

The kind where masks come off.

The kind where they stop performing strength and finally become emotionally honest.

Some women discover that although they cannot recover lost years, they can still recover themselves.

And that matters.

Because becoming whole is greater than simply becoming married.

- Marriage does not heal broken people.
- Children do not heal broken people.
- Relationships do not heal broken people.
- Only true healing heals broken people.

Some women spent their younger years chasing love without ever becoming healthy enough to sustain it once it arrived.

Others kept searching for "the right man" while never allowing God to address the wrong things within themselves.

And sometimes the hardest truth to face is this:

Not every closed door was bad luck.

Some doors closed because unresolved brokenness made lasting love impossible.

Yet God is still merciful!

- Even after years of mistakes.
- Even after decades of emotional damage.
- Even after isolation, pride, rebellion, fear, trauma, or poor decisions.

Healing is still possible.
Wholeness is still possible.
Peace is still possible.

But it begins with truth.

Not blame.
Not denial.
Not pretending.
Not hiding behind independence.

Truth.

Because until a person becomes honest about what is broken, they will spend their entire life calling dysfunction "personality" while wondering why nothing ever changes.

Chapter 6

Wounds That Run Deep

Some wounds are visible.

You can see the scars.
You can see the bruises.
You can see the damage.

But some of the deepest wounds a human being can carry are the ones nobody ever sees.

Molestation.
Sexual assault.
Rape.

These experiences do not simply hurt the body. They invade the mind, distort emotions, fracture trust, and alter the way many survivors see themselves, relationships, love, intimacy, safety, and even their own value.

They create access for the enemy to enter and set up shop in the shadows of their life, undetected.

And when the violation comes from a parent, sibling, uncle, aunt, cousin, grandparent, or trusted family member, the damage often cuts even deeper.

Because the very people who were supposed to provide protection became the source of the trauma.

That kind of betrayal changes a person internally in ways many people cannot fully understand.

A child naturally believes family equals safety. A child depends emotionally, mentally, and physically on those closest to them. So when a trusted relative violates that boundary, the child's mind often cannot fully process what is happening.

Many survivors become confused before they ever become angry.

Some children do not even realize they were abused until years later. Others knew something was wrong but were manipulated into silence through fear, threats, guilt, gifts, or emotional control.

Some were told:

"This is our secret."
"Nobody will believe you."
"You wanted this."
"You'll destroy this family if you tell."
"This is how people show love."

Those words become psychological chains.

The abuse itself is traumatic. But the manipulation attached to it often creates lifelong emotional confusion.

Many survivors of family sexual abuse grow up struggling with identity, self-worth, emotional regulation, and trust because the people who taught them what "love" looked like also taught them pain, fear, secrecy, and violation.

That confusion can follow them into adulthood.

A woman violated by her father, stepfather, brother, uncle, or cousin may later struggle with trusting men altogether. She may desire love deeply while simultaneously fearing closeness. She may crave emotional intimacy but panic when someone gets too close emotionally or physically.

Some become emotionally detached.
Others become overly attached.

Some find comfort in same-sex relationships.
While others avoid relationships entirely.

Others constantly seek validation through relationships or sex.
Many become promiscuous.

Many survivors battle anxiety without understanding its true root.

Their nervous systems learned early that safety could disappear at any moment.

So even years later, they may live in a constant state of emotional alertness. They overthink conversations. They expect betrayal. They struggle to relax emotionally. Some become controlling because control makes them feel safer. Others emotionally shut down because vulnerability feels dangerous.

The body often remembers trauma even when the mind tries to bury it.

A smell.
A tone of voice.
A certain touch.
A room.
A song.
A phrase.

Triggers can reopen emotions years after the abuse stopped.

Many survivors also struggle with shame.

Not because they were guilty, but because trauma often convinces victims that something about them is damaged, dirty, broken, or unworthy.

This is especially true when the abuse happened repeatedly over years.

A child who is repeatedly violated by someone close to them often begins internalizing destructive beliefs:

"I must not matter."
"My boundaries do not matter."
"I exist to be used."
"Love always comes with pain."
"I cannot trust anyone."
"My voice does not matter."

Those beliefs quietly shape adult behavior.

A man who was molested as a boy may grow up angry, emotionally numb, hypersexual, withdrawn, addicted, depressed, or deeply insecure while never fully understanding why.

Many men never tell anyone what happened to them.

Some fear embarrassment.
Some fear appearing weak.
Some fear judgment.
Some were told that because they were male, they should have enjoyed it.
Others fear being questioned about their masculinity or identity.

So they bury it.

But buried trauma does not disappear.

It leaks into relationships, marriages, parenting, communication, emotional regulation, and self-worth.

Some men become emotionally disconnected because vulnerability reminds them of powerlessness. Others become aggressive because anger feels safer than pain. Some become addicted to pornography, sex, alcohol, drugs, or constant distractions because numbing the pain feels easier than confronting it.

And many become masters at pretending they are fine.

Successful on the outside.
Broken internally.

One of the deepest psychological effects of family sexual abuse is confusion surrounding love and trust.

When the people closest to someone become the source of pain, the mind often struggles to separate love from danger.

As adults, many survivors unconsciously attract or tolerate unhealthy relationships because dysfunction feels familiar. Chaos can feel more normal than peace. Some survivors repeatedly choose emotionally unavailable, controlling, manipulative, or abusive partners because their understanding of love was damaged early in life.

Others sabotage healthy relationships because healthy love feels unfamiliar and unsafe.

Sometimes survivors push good people away before they can get hurt again.
Sometimes they become suspicious of everyone.
Sometimes they struggle with physical affection because touch no longer feels emotionally safe.
Some survivors dissociate emotionally during intimacy. Others become hypersexual because sex became psychologically connected to validation, control, attention, or acceptance.

Trauma affects people differently.

There is no single response.

Some become quiet.
Some become loud.
Some become hyper-sexual.
Some become fearful of intimacy.

Some become perfectionists.
Some struggle with self-harm.
Some develop eating disorders.
Some battle severe anxiety or depression.
Some become emotionally cold simply to survive internally.

And many spend years pretending the abuse "didn't affect them."

But unresolved trauma almost always surfaces eventually.

In relationships.
In communication.
In parenting.
In emotional triggers.
In trust issues.
In anger.
In fear.
In insecurity.
In emotional instability.

The pain eventually speaks.

One of the most heartbreaking realities is that some survivors were never protected after speaking up.

Some were ignored.
Some were blamed.
Some were called liars.
Some families protected the abuser to "keep peace."
Some survivors were told not to "destroy the family."
Some watched relatives pretend nothing ever happened.

That secondary betrayal often deepens the trauma even more than the abuse itself.

Because now the survivor not only feels violated… they feel abandoned.

Many survivors grow up carrying silent rage toward parents who failed to protect them. Others feel guilt for exposing the abuse. Some still love the family member who violated them, which creates emotional confusion and shame.

Trauma inside families is rarely simple emotionally.

Healing from these wounds usually requires honesty.

Not pretending.
Not minimizing.
Not masking pain behind religion, relationships, success, sex, or accomplishments.

Real healing begins when survivors finally acknowledge:

"What happened to me deeply affected me."

That truth can break years of denial.

Healing is not weakness.

Seeking counseling is not weakness.
Talking about trauma is not weakness.
Setting boundaries is not weakness.
Admitting pain is not weakness.

Many survivors spent their entire childhood surviving emotionally. As adults, they finally have to learn how to truly heal.

Healing does not erase the past.

But it can stop the past from controlling the future.

And healing is rarely instant.

Some wounds heal in layers.
Some memories resurface unexpectedly.
Some triggers remain for years.

But healing is still possible.

A survivor is not permanently worthless because they were violated.

They are not dirty.
They are not ruined.
They are not beyond love.
They are not beyond peace.
They are not beyond healthy relationships.

What happened to them matters deeply.

But what happened to them does not have to become their permanent identity.

Some people spend their lives running from the pain.

Others spend their lives pretending the pain never existed.

But true healing begins when someone finally stops hiding from the wound and confronts it honestly.

Because the silent wounds always speak eventually.

Chapter 7
Living in Denial

One of the most dangerous aspects of brokenness is not the wound itself.

It is denial.

Many people are not only wounded.
They are committed to protecting the illusion that they are fine.

Denial is what allows brokenness to survive for years while convincing the person they are healthy.

Some people deny through pride.
Others through blame.
Others through busyness.
Others through religion.
Others through relationships.
Others through anger.
Others through silence.

But regardless of the method, denial protects dysfunction from exposure.

And whatever remains hidden remains empowered.

Many broken people become masters at rationalizing unhealthy behavior.

The angry man says:
"That's just how I talk."

The controlling woman says:
"If I don't control things, everything falls apart."

The emotionally detached husband says:
"I'm just not emotional."

The prideful leader says:
"People just don't understand me."

The manipulative person says:
"I only did that because they hurt me first."

The wounded individual rarely sees their behavior as broken.

They see it as justified.

This is one reason brokenness becomes so dangerous.

Pain distorts perception.

People no longer see themselves clearly.

Instead of confronting wounds honestly, many spend years building arguments around why they should remain unchanged.

Some normalize rage because they were raised around rage.

Some normalize emotional neglect because they never experienced healthy affection.

Some normalize chaos because peace feels unfamiliar.

Some normalize lust because sexual perversion became common early in life.

Some normalize manipulation because manipulation was modeled throughout childhood.

Brokenness repeated long enough eventually feels normal.

And when dysfunction becomes familiar, truth begins feeling offensive.

This is why many broken people react strongly when confronted honestly. They become angry and confrontation.

Correction threatens denial.

Accountability threatens self-protection.

Truth threatens the false identity they carefully built around survival.

Some people secretly know they are broken.

But they fear what healing would require.

Healing would require ***humility***.

It would require admitting:
"I am not okay."

For many people, those words feel unbearable.

Especially when their entire identity has been built around appearing strong, spiritual, successful, intelligent, independent, or emotionally unaffected.

Denial often becomes strongest in people who spent years surviving.

Because survival taught them:
- Never appear weak
- Never trust fully
- Never expose pain
- Never let people see vulnerability
- Never lose control

Eventually survival mode becomes permanent.

And the person no longer knows how to live honestly.

Some people are emotionally exhausted not because healing is unavailable, but because pretending is exhausting.

Maintaining masks requires constant effort.

Pretending to be unbothered.
Pretending to be strong.
Pretending to be happy.
Pretending to be spiritually mature.
Pretending not to care.
Pretending not to hurt.

Denial becomes a prison disguised as protection.

One of the clearest signs of denial is defensiveness.

Broken people often protect wounds aggressively.

Not because they are evil.

But because exposed wounds feel threatening.

A simple correction can trigger disproportionate anger because the person feels exposed internally.

A spouse bringing up emotional distance suddenly becomes:
"You always criticize me."

A friend confronting unhealthy behavior becomes:
"You think you're better than me."

A pastor addressing hidden sin becomes:
"People are judging me."

Why?

Because denial interprets exposure as attack.

Pride immediately moves to defend the image.

Another sign of denial is blame shifting.

Many broken people become experts at explaining why everyone else is responsible for their condition.

Their spouse.
Their parents.
Their childhood.
Their church.
Their ex-spouse.
Society.
Leadership.
Friends.

While wounds are real, healing cannot begin until responsibility enters the picture.

A person cannot control what happened to them.

But eventually they must confront what they are becoming because of it.

Some people remain emotionally bound because blaming others feels safer than confronting themselves.

Denial also appears through emotional suppression.

Many people are not emotionally stable.

They are emotionally numb.

There is a difference.

Some have buried grief so deeply they no longer know how to feel tenderness.
Some buried rejection beneath pride.
Some buried fear beneath control.
Some buried insecurity beneath arrogance.
Some buried pain beneath lust, addictions, entertainment, work, or constant distraction.

But buried pain does not disappear.

It waits.

Eventually unresolved heart wounds begin leaking into behavior, relationships, decision-making, emotional reactions, and spiritual health.

The Bible says in Proverbs 4:23 (NIV): *Above all else, guard your heart, for everything you do flows from it.*

Guard it from pride, fear, isolation, bitterness and unforgiveness.

This is why some people explode emotionally over small situations.

The reaction is rarely about the moment itself. Rather, unresolved issues.

The moment simply touched an unhealed heart wound.

A man erupts with rage over feeling disrespected because deep inside he still carries unresolved rejection and insecurity.

A woman becomes emotionally controlling because abandonment still lives inside her fearfully.

A person withdraws emotionally after conflict because vulnerability feels unsafe due to earlier heart wounds.

Brokenness rarely stays isolated.

It spills.

This is also why many people struggle receiving truth spiritually.

Denial hardens the heart.

When people repeatedly justify sin, dysfunction, pride, sexual perversion, bitterness, manipulation, lust, unforgiveness, or emotional brokenness, they slowly become resistant to conviction.

What once bothered their conscience no longer affects them.

This is spiritually dangerous.

Because one of the most frightening stages of brokenness is when bondage starts feeling normal.

Some people become so accustomed to chaos that peace feels uncomfortable.

Some become so accustomed to dysfunction that healthy relationships feel boring.

Some become so accustomed to survival mode that resting feels unsafe.

Some become so accustomed to emotional walls that intimacy feels threatening.

Denial convinces people they are protecting themselves.

But often they are protecting the very thing destroying them.

This is where spiritual deception becomes powerful.

The enemy often reinforces denial by feeding lies such as:
"You're fine."
"It's them, not you."
"Everybody struggles like this."

"This is just your personality."
"You can't change."
"You don't have to change."
"Nobody would love the real you."
"You don't need help."
"People are just trying to control you."
"You're the victim in every situation."

Over time these lies become internal agreements.

And agreements create strongholds. And strongholds create contracts. And contracts produce cycles and generational curses.

This is why some people sabotage every healthy relationship they encounter.

Not because they consciously desire destruction.

But because healthy love threatens unhealthy identities.

Healing threatens the version of themselves built around pain.

Many broken people fear healing more than suffering.

Because suffering is familiar.
Healing is unknown.

Real healing requires surrender.

It requires honesty without excuses.
It requires humility without performance.
It requires accountability without defensiveness.
It requires confronting hidden pride, hidden fear, hidden bitterness, hidden lust, hidden insecurity, hidden shame, and hidden pain.

Most importantly, it requires truth.

Because denial survives through deception.

But freedom begins the moment a person finally becomes honest about their condition.

Chapter 8

The Spiritual Nature of Brokenness

Many people acknowledge emotional brokenness.

Far fewer acknowledge spiritual brokenness.

Modern culture has become comfortable discussing trauma, personality disorders, emotional wounds, unhealthy attachment styles, behavioral patterns, anxiety, depression, insecurity, and coping mechanisms. People are increasingly willing to admit emotional pain exists.

It has been increasingly easier to lump everything under "mental illness."

But many still resist the reality that brokenness is not merely emotional.

It is spiritual.

There is an unseen war taking place within people.

A war involving truth and deception.
Light and darkness.
Freedom and bondage.
The Spirit and the flesh.

Some people attempt to explain every destructive behavior psychologically while completely ignoring the spiritual dimension operating underneath it.

Others swing to the opposite extreme and blame every struggle entirely on demons while avoiding personal responsibility, repentance, discipline, and accountability.

Both extremes miss truth.

Brokenness is often deeply spiritual because heart wounds, sin, pride, trauma, bitterness, lust, rebellion, fear, and unforgiveness can become open doors for spiritual bondage.

Not every struggle is demonic.

But unresolved brokenness creates vulnerability to demonic access.

The enemy studies wounds.

He studies:
Rejection.
Fear.
Abandonment.
Trauma.
Shame.
Pride.
Isolation.
Bitterness.
Sexual brokenness.
Insecurity.

Why?

Because wounded places are often the easiest places to influence.

A rejected child may become an adult who secretly believes:
"I am unworthy of love."

An abandoned person may believe:
"Everyone eventually leaves."

A wounded man may believe:
"Vulnerability is weakness."

A betrayed woman may believe:
"Control is the only way to stay safe."

At first these may seem like simple emotional conclusions.

But over time these lies become spiritual agreements.

And agreements with lies become strongholds.

A stronghold is more than behavior.

It is spiritual influence or possession that fortifies a pattern of thinking and behavior that opposes truth and keeps a person spiritually, emotionally, and mentally bound.

The enemy does not need to visibly possess someone to influence them.

If he can keep a person trapped in deception, pride, fear, lust, rage, shame, bitterness, insecurity, or self-hatred, he can quietly influence the direction of their life for years.

Many people imagine demonic influence only as dramatic manifestations.

Hollywood images.
Violent outbursts.
Extreme possession.

But often spiritual bondage appears far more subtle.

Sometimes it looks like:
- Chronic rage
- Constant chaos
- Tormenting thoughts
- Addictions
- Sexual bondage
- Deep confusion
- Emotional instability
- Self-hatred
- Persistent fear
- Isolation
- Compulsive destruction
- Pride that rejects correction
- Inability to maintain peace
- Repeated cycles of sabotage

Some people repeatedly destroy healthy relationships while claiming they simply "have bad luck."

Some cannot maintain peace no matter how much success they gain externally.

Some constantly feel empty even after achieving what they once believed would satisfy them.

Others secretly battle tormenting thoughts they cannot escape.

Brokenness becomes spiritual when lies become identity.

This is why unresolved heart wounds are dangerous.

A heart wound by itself is painful.

But a heart wound combined with deception becomes bondage.

For example:
A woman rejected by her father may begin believing:
"I am unwanted."

That belief affects how she dates, trusts, receives love, handles conflict, responds emotionally, and sees herself.

Over time she may unknowingly attract relationships that reinforce the lie already living within her because the enemy knows exactly what to send her way.

A man humiliated repeatedly growing up may build his entire identity around power, pride, aggression, money, or control to avoid ever feeling weak again.

But underneath the image is still the wounded child trying to protect himself.

Many addictions are not rooted merely in pleasure.

They are rooted in pain.

Some people are not addicted because they love destruction.

They are addicted because they are attempting to medicate wounds they never healed from.

Lust often becomes escape.
Drugs become escape.
Alcohol becomes escape.
Pornography becomes escape.

Work becomes escape.
Attention becomes escape.

People often run toward bondage searching for relief.

But bondage never heals pain.

It deepens it.

This is why sin and brokenness often become spiritually connected.

Repeated sin hardens the heart.

And hardened hearts become easier to deceive.

Pride especially creates dangerous spiritual blindness.

Pride convinces people:
- "I'm fine."
- "I don't need help."
- "Everyone else is the problem."
- "Nobody can correct me."
- "I already know."
- "I can handle this myself."

Pride resists surrender.

And whatever resists surrender resists healing.

This is why some people remain bound for years despite hearing truth repeatedly.

Truth cannot free a person committed to protecting deception.

Spiritual bondage also grows in hidden places.

Unforgiveness hidden for years.
Secret lust.
Hidden hatred.
Private addictions.
Chronic bitterness.
Jealousy.
Manipulation.
Pride.
Rebellion.

Darkness survives where truth is resisted.

Some people unknowingly build entire lifestyles around protecting spiritual strongholds.

They protect the anger because anger makes them feel powerful.
They protect the pride because vulnerability terrifies them.
They protect the addiction because sobriety would force them to confront pain honestly.
They protect the control because surrender feels unsafe.

The frightening reality is that many people no longer recognize bondage because bondage has become familiar.

Chaos feels normal.
Fear feels normal.
Lust feels normal.
Emotional instability feels normal.
Isolation feels normal.
Constant mental torment feels normal, (they say they can't sleep at night, their brain is always racing).

This is one reason deliverance can feel threatening to broken people.

Freedom requires the destruction of false identities.

It requires exposing lies.

It requires surrendering the version of themselves built around pain, pride, fear, control, lust, or bitterness.

Many people want relief without surrender.

But freedom does not come merely through emotional moments.

It comes through truth.

Real deliverance is not performance.

It is transformation.

It is not merely screaming prayers, emotional experiences, or dramatic manifestations.

True deliverance involves:
- Repentance
- Truth
- Humility
- Gratitude
- Renouncing lies
- Forgiveness
- Surrender
- Renewing the mind
- Breaking agreement with darkness

- Canceling contracts with darness
- Submitting fully to God
- Walking consistently in truth

A person cannot continually feed darkness while expecting freedom from darkness.

Healing requires cooperation with truth.

This is why some people experience temporary emotional breakthroughs yet remain unchanged afterward.

The emotional moment occurred.

But the agreement with lies remained intact.

Real freedom happens when truth replaces deception at the root.

When identity is restored.
When pride is surrendered.
When wounds are confronted honestly.
When forgiveness replaces bitterness.
When humility replaces self-protection.
When gratitude replaces selfishness.
When peace replaces chaos.
When God's truth becomes greater than the lies pain created.

The enemy wants wounded people to remain trapped in shame, secrecy, fear, pride, addiction, and hopelessness.

Why?

Because broken people often reproduce brokenness.

Hurt people hurt people.

Bound fathers wound children.
Bound mothers wound families.
Bound leaders wound churches.
Bound individuals wound relationships.

But freedom interrupts cycles.
Healing interrupts generational bondage.

Truth destroys lies.

And light exposes what darkness spent years hiding.

The spiritual nature of brokenness cannot be ignored.

Because many people are not only emotionally wounded.

They are spiritually imprisoned and calling it personality.

Chapter 9
When Bondage Feels Normal

One of the most dangerous stages of brokenness is when dysfunction no longer feels dysfunctional.

When chaos becomes familiar.
When torment becomes routine.
When fear becomes personality.
When pride becomes protection.
When lust becomes normal.
When anger becomes identity.
When emotional distance becomes comfort.

Bondage becomes most powerful when the person no longer recognizes they are bound.

Many people are not fighting their chains anymore.

They have adapted to them.

At first brokenness usually feels uncomfortable.

A person notices:
The instability.
The emotional reactions.
The fear.
The insecurity.
The rage.
The emptiness.
The compulsive behaviors.

But over time, repeated exposure creates normalization.

The person slowly adjusts to living wounded.

Eventually they stop asking:
"Why am I like this?"

Now they say:
"This is just who I am."

That sentence has imprisoned countless people spiritually and emotionally.

Some people have been angry for so long they no longer know what peace feels like. They are deceived in to thinking they are at peace but have nerves issues and get easily agitated when talking about what they're guarding.

Some have been anxious for so long that calmness feels unfamiliar.

Some have lived in survival mode for decades and cannot relax even when danger is absent.

Some have been emotionally disconnected for so long that intimacy feels threatening instead of safe.

Some have hidden behind pride for so many years that humility feels humiliating.

Bondage becomes normal through repetition.

This is how generational brokenness survives.

A child raised around screaming eventually sees rage as normal communication.

A child raised around manipulation begins seeing control as love.

A boy raised without affection may grow into a man incapable of expressing tenderness because emotional distance feels natural to him.

A girl raised around emotional inconsistency may later confuse instability with passion.

What is repeated consistently becomes familiar.

And familiarity often disguises bondage.

This is why some people repeatedly enter destructive relationships.

Not because they consciously desire pain.

But because dysfunction feels recognizable.

Healthy love often feels uncomfortable to broken people because peace exposes how chaotic they have become internally.

A man accustomed to toxic relationships may become suspicious of a peaceful woman because drama feels more emotionally familiar than stability.

A woman raised around emotional inconsistency may feel emotionally unstimulated by healthy consistency because her nervous system became conditioned to chaos.

Brokenness trains people to feel "at home" inside unhealthy environments.

This is one reason many wounded individuals sabotage healthy relationships.

Not because they hate love.

But because healthy love threatens unhealthy identity patterns.

Some people do not know how to function:

Without chaos.
Without conflict.
Without control.
Without emotional games.
Without manipulation.
Without instability.

Peace feels foreign.

And whatever feels foreign often feels unsafe to broken people.

This same pattern exists spiritually.

Many people become so accustomed to spiritual heaviness, torment, fear, condemnation, lust, confusion, emotional instability, or addiction that they stop believing freedom is possible.

They settle into survival.

Some believers secretly live their entire lives battling hidden bondage while publicly pretending everything is fine.

The addicted worship leader.
The rage-filled husband.
The manipulative wife.
The prideful preacher.
The secretly depressed leader.
The emotionally detached father.
The woman consumed with insecurity while presenting confidence externally.

Many are functioning publicly while suffering privately.

And because the bondage has existed so long, they begin identifying with it.

Instead of saying:
"I am battling fear."

They now say:
"I'm just an anxious person."

Instead of:
"I need healing from rejection."

They say:
"I just don't trust people."

Instead of:
"I struggle with control because of unresolved heart wounds."

They say:
"That's just my personality."

Brokenness becomes identity when bondage feels normal.

This is one reason spiritual strongholds become so difficult to break.

The person no longer sees the issue as something affecting them.

They see it as who they are.

And people fiercely protect identities.

Even destructive ones.

This is why truth often creates strong emotional reactions in wounded individuals.

Truth threatens normalization.

It threatens the false peace people built around dysfunction.

Some people become angry when confronted because deep inside they know the truth is exposing something they spent years protecting.

Others immediately withdraw emotionally.
Others mock truth.
Others rationalize behavior.
Others become defensive.
Others blame everyone around them.

All because bondage fights exposure.

Darkness prefers familiarity.

The enemy wants people comfortable with dysfunction.

Comfortable with pornography.
Comfortable with rage.
Comfortable with bitterness.
Comfortable with emotional manipulation.
Comfortable with pride.
Comfortable with lust.
Comfortable with fear.
Comfortable with compromise.

Why?

Because normalized bondage rarely gets confronted.

Many people stay trapped because ***everyone around them shares the same dysfunction.***

Entire friend groups normalize sexual immorality.
Entire families normalize rage.
Entire churches normalize pride and performance.
Entire cultures normalize emotional brokenness while calling it empowerment, independence, masculinity, confidence, or freedom.

But normalization never transforms dysfunction into health.

Darkness remains darkness even when culture celebrates it.

This is why some people become uncomfortable around truly healed individuals.

Healed people expose unhealthy patterns without even trying.

A peaceful person exposes chaos.
A humble person exposes pride.

An emotionally healthy person exposes manipulation.
A disciplined person exposes compromise.
A transparent person exposes performance.

Sometimes broken people resent healed people because healing confronts what they refuse to address within themselves.

The frightening reality is that many people become addicted to the very thing destroying them.

Some become addicted to chaos.
Some addicted to attention.
Some addicted to victimhood.
Some addicted to emotional instability.
Some addicted to lust.
Some addicted to anger because anger makes them feel powerful.
Some addicted to control because surrender terrifies them.

Bondage survives wherever pain remains unconfronted honestly.

This is why true healing requires more than behavior modification.

A person can temporarily change actions while remaining internally bound.

Real freedom reaches identity.

It changes how a person:
Thinks.
Responds.
Loves.
Trusts.
Handles conflict.
Receives correction.
Experiences peace.
Sees themselves.

Healing is not merely removing bad habits.

It is restoring truth where lies once ruled.

This is also why many people experience temporary breakthroughs but later return to old patterns.

The environment changed briefly.

The emotions changed briefly.

But the identity remained unchanged.

And whatever identity remains unchanged eventually pulls the person back toward familiar bondage.

People always drift toward what feels normal internally.

This is why renewing the mind is essential.

Because freedom requires learning what healthy actually looks like.

Some people genuinely do not know.

They never witnessed:
Healthy love.
Healthy communication.
Healthy masculinity.
Healthy femininity.
Healthy parenting.
Healthy conflict resolution.
Healthy emotional expression.

Brokenness was all they ever knew.

So healing often feels unnatural in the beginning.

Peace feels strange.
Boundaries feel uncomfortable.
Consistency feels boring.

Transparency feels vulnerable.
Rest feels unsafe.
Humility feels weak.

But many things that feel uncomfortable initially are actually evidence of healing beginning.

Freedom often feels unfamiliar before it feels peaceful.

This is why healing requires persistence.

A person must stop romanticizing dysfunction.

Stop defending bondage.

Stop calling brokenness personality.

And stop treating chains like comfort.

Because what people normalize eventually controls them.

And many people are living in prisons they no longer recognize because bondage became familiar long ago.

Chapter 10

PRIDE — The Protector of Brokenness

Pride is one of the most powerful and misunderstood forces operating inside wounded people.

Most people imagine pride as arrogance.

Loudness.
Boasting.
Self-importance.
Dominance.

But some of the most prideful individuals appear quiet, humble, calm, or even deeply spiritual externally.

Because pride is not always visible confidence.

Sometimes pride is self-protection.
Sometimes pride is the armor broken people wear to prevent anyone from touching the heart wounds beneath the surface.

Many people do not realize that pride often develops after pain.

A person who was humiliated may build pride to avoid ever feeling weak again.

A rejected person may build pride to avoid needing anyone emotionally.

A betrayed individual may build pride because vulnerability now feels dangerous.

A wounded man may become emotionally hard because softness reminds him of pain.

A wounded woman may become controlling because surrender feels unsafe.

Pride often begins as protection.

But eventually protection becomes prison.

Broken people often use pride to preserve image rather than pursue healing.

Because healing requires exposure.

And exposure terrifies wounded people.

Pride says:
“Hide it.”

Pride says:
“Protect yourself.”

Pride says:
“Never let them see weakness.”

Pride says:
“Stay in control.”

Pride says:
“Never admit you were wrong.”

Pride says:
“Don’t apologize.”

Pride says:
“Defend yourself at all costs.”

This is why pride is so dangerous spiritually and emotionally.

It resists the very things healing requires.

Healing requires humility.
Healing requires honesty.
Healing requires accountability.
Healing requires surrender.
Healing requires gratitude.

But pride fights all five.

Many broken people are not difficult because they are evil.

They are difficult because pride has become the guardian of their heart wounds.

Pride stands at the entrance of brokenness like a bodyguard refusing entry to truth.

This is why some people react aggressively and become confrontational to correction.

Not because the correction is inaccurate.

But because correction threatens the identity they built around survival.

A simple conversation suddenly becomes defensiveness.

A loving encounter becomes an argument.

Accountability becomes "judgment."

Truth becomes "disrespect."

The wounded soul immediately interprets exposure as attack.

Why?

Because pride survives through self-preservation.

Some people would rather destroy relationships than admit they are wrong.

Others would rather isolate themselves than become vulnerable.

Others silently punish people emotionally because humility feels unbearable to them.

Pride convinces people that vulnerability is weakness.

But vulnerability is often the doorway to healing.

Many wounded individuals have become experts at performance.

Performing strength.
Performing peace.
Performing spirituality.
Performing confidence.
Performing emotional stability.

But performance is exhausting.

Because pretending requires constant maintenance.

Some people are not emotionally healthy.

They are emotionally guarded.

There is a difference.

A healed person can be transparent without collapsing internally.

A prideful person constantly manages perception.

Everything becomes image protection.

How they are viewed.
How they are perceived.
How they appear spiritually.
How they appear emotionally.
How they appear socially.

Pride becomes a mask hiding insecurity.

This is why some people cannot apologize sincerely. An apology feels like loss of control.

Others cannot receive correction without becoming defensive.
Others constantly blame everyone around them.
Others weaponize silence.
Others manipulate conversations to avoid accountability.
Others become experts at pointing out flaws in everyone except themselves.

Why?

Because pride survives by redirecting exposure.

As long as attention stays on everyone else, the wounded person never has to confront themselves honestly.

This is why pride and brokenness often become deeply intertwined.

Pride protects the heart wound while simultaneously preventing healing from reaching it.

The frightening reality is that pride can exist inside highly religious people.

Some people know scripture while remaining emotionally toxic.
Some pray publicly while secretly battling rage privately.
Some preach forgiveness while feeding bitterness for years.
Some appear spiritually mature while remaining emotionally immature.

Religious activity can become camouflage for unresolved brokenness.

A person may:
- attend church faithfully
- serve consistently
- quote scripture fluently
- worship passionately

While still being controlled by:
- insecurity
- manipulation
- control
- pride
- lust
- fear
- anger
- hidden torment

Because activity is not transformation.

Noise is not healing.

Emotion is not deliverance.

Many people have learned how to perform spirituality while remaining internally fractured.

This is one reason pride is so dangerous.

Pride convinces people they are healed because they appear functional.

But functionality is not freedom.

A man can provide financially while remaining emotionally unavailable.

A woman can appear nurturing while manipulating everyone emotionally behind closed doors.

A leader can inspire crowds while secretly being consumed with insecurity and fear of exposure.

Brokenness often survives beneath outward success.

And pride works tirelessly to keep it hidden.

Pride also keeps many people trapped in cycles for years.

Because pride resists repentance.

True repentance is not merely saying:
"I'm sorry."

True repentance requires honesty.

It requires humility.

It requires the willingness to confront darkness within yourself without excuses, blame shifting, or self-protection.

But pride fears self-examination.

Why?

Because many wounded individuals built entire identities around appearing strong.

Some men were taught:
Never cry.
Never show weakness.
Never admit fear.
Never appear vulnerable.

Some women learned:
Never trust fully.
Never depend emotionally.
Never let people too close.
Never appear needy.

Over time survival mechanisms become personality.
And pride becomes deeply woven into identity.

Eventually the person no longer knows who they are:

Without the walls.
Without control.
Without emotional distance.
Without self-protection.

This is why healing feels threatening for many wounded individuals.

Because healing requires dismantling false versions of themselves.

It requires laying down the mask.
It requires exposure.
It requires surrender.

And surrender terrifies pride.

But pride cannot heal what it refuses to expose.

Hidden wounds continue influencing:
- relationships
- decisions
- emotional reactions
- parenting
- intimacy
- trust
- spiritual health
- identity

Many broken people are not merely battling pain.
They are battling the fear of being seen.
The fear that if someone truly saw them, they would be rejected.

So pride builds walls.

Walls of anger.
Walls of silence.
Walls of control.
Walls of independence.
Walls of performance.
Walls of emotional detachment.

But walls that keep pain out also keep healing out.

This is why humility is so powerful spiritually.

Humility tears down the false image.
Humility allows honesty.
Humility invites transformation.

Humility says:
"I need help."
"I am not okay."
"I cannot heal myself."
"I need God to confront what I have hidden."

Pride says:
"I'm fine."

Even while internally collapsing.

Many people remain emotionally exhausted because pride forces them to maintain an image they were never meant to carry.

Pretending becomes heavy.

Performing becomes draining.

Survival becomes exhausting.

And eventually the soul begins craving freedom more than image protection.

This is often where healing finally begins.

Not when the person becomes perfect.

But when they become honest.

Because healing begins where pride ends.

Chapter 11

The Man Who Uses Silence

Not all brokenness is loud.

Some broken people explode.

Others disappear.

Some scream.
Others shut down.

Some create chaos openly.
Others create it quietly.

One of the most misunderstood forms of brokenness is silence.

Not peaceful silence.
Not healthy reflection.

But silence used as protection, punishment, control, avoidance, or emotional withdrawal.

Many people mistake silence for strength because it appears calm externally.

But silence can become one of the most emotionally damaging weapons wounded people use.

Especially in relationships.

Some people learned very early that emotions were unsafe.

Unsafe to express.
Unsafe to reveal.
Unsafe to trust with others.

So instead of learning healthy communication, they learned emotional shutdown.

Some learned it from harsh fathers.

Others from emotionally unavailable mothers.

Others from homes filled with criticism, conflict, instability, manipulation, or rejection.

A child who repeatedly felt unheard may eventually stop speaking honestly altogether.

A child who was mocked emotionally may later associate vulnerability with humiliation.

A boy repeatedly taught:
"Man up."
"Stop crying."
"Don't be weak."

may eventually disconnect from his emotions entirely.

Over time silence becomes survival.

The person no longer processes emotions honestly.

They suppress them.

But suppressed emotions do not disappear.

They bury themselves beneath the surface where they quietly influence behavior, relationships, intimacy, trust, and emotional stability.

Many emotionally silent people are not calm internally.

They are overwhelmed internally.

But instead of communicating pain, fear, insecurity, disappointment, rejection, sadness, confusion, or anger honestly, they retreat emotionally.

Silence becomes their hiding place.

Some men use silence because they fear confrontation emotionally.

Others use silence because they fear exposure.

Others because they never learned emotional language.

Others because shutting down gives them a sense of control.

And for some, silence becomes punishment.

The wounded person withdraws emotionally after conflict, forcing everyone around them to carry the emotional tension while they remain distant.

To outsiders they may appear composed.

But emotional shutdown is not peace.

Distance is not maturity.

Withdrawal is not emotional strength.

Some people use silence to avoid accountability.

As long as they refuse to communicate honestly, they never have to confront what is actually happening inside them.

Silence protects pride.
Silence protects fear.
Silence protects insecurity.
Silence protects heart wounds.

But silence also slowly destroys intimacy.

Because intimacy cannot survive emotional absence.

A relationship may continue externally while emotionally dying internally.

Two people may share a house while living emotionally disconnected for years.

Conversations become surface-level.

Affection becomes mechanical.

Conflict becomes unresolved tension.

And eventually loneliness enters the relationship even while both people remain physically present.

This is one reason emotionally unavailable people often confuse providing with connecting.

They believe:
"I work."
"I provide."
"I stay faithful."
"I handle responsibilities."

while never realizing emotional presence is also necessary for healthy relationships.

A person can remain physically present while emotionally absent.

And emotional absence creates deep wounds over time.

Many women carrying emotional exhaustion in relationships are not exhausted by a lack of provision.

They are exhausted by emotional disconnection.

Likewise, many men silently carry emotional wounds because they feel unseen, disrespected, rejected, or emotionally unsafe but never learned how to express those feelings honestly.

Instead they retreat into silence.

But silence rarely heals what caused the pain.

It usually deepens it.

Some people convince themselves:
"If I avoid talking about it, eventually it will disappear."

But buried pain does not disappear.

It waits.

And eventually it leaks into:
- irritability
- emotional distance
- resentment
- passive aggression
- coldness
- lust
- infidelity
- addictions
- anger
- emotional numbness

Many emotionally silent individuals are carrying years of unresolved pain they never processed honestly.

Some are silently carrying rejection.

Others betrayal.
Others shame.
Others fear.
Others feelings of inadequacy.
Others childhood heart wounds.
Others resentment they never released.

And because the wounds remain hidden, they continue affecting every relationship the person enters.

Silence also creates confusion inside relationships.

The emotionally connected person often feels trapped trying to interpret what the silent person is actually feeling.

Are they angry?
Hurt?
Disconnected?
Punishing?
Overwhelmed?
Afraid?
Ashamed?

The silence creates emotional instability because unresolved tension leaves people emotionally guessing.

This is why emotional shutdown can become manipulative even when unintended.

The silent person controls the emotional atmosphere without communicating honestly.

Everyone around them:
Feels the distance.
Feels the tension.
Feels the disconnection.

But receives no clarity.

This often leaves the other person emotionally anxious, frustrated, insecure, or exhausted.

Some wounded individuals learned silence because conflict in childhood felt dangerous.

So now, instead of confronting issues honestly, they withdraw entirely.

Others use silence because vulnerability feels terrifying.

Talking honestly would require exposure.

And exposure threatens the image they built around appearing strong.

Some people can discuss business, sports, politics, money, leadership, or theology for hours while remaining incapable of expressing simple emotional truth.

Truth like:
"I'm hurt."
"I'm afraid."
"I feel rejected."
"I don't know how to communicate."
"I need help."
"I don't feel safe emotionally."
"I never learned how to process this."

Why?

Because emotional honesty feels more threatening than silence.

Silence allows wounded people to hide behind control.

But hidden emotions continue shaping behavior regardless of whether they are acknowledged.

Many emotionally distant people secretly crave intimacy while simultaneously fearing it.

They want connection.

But connection requires vulnerability.

And vulnerability threatens the walls they built to survive.

So they remain trapped between desire and fear.

Wanting closeness.
But fearing exposure.

Wanting love.
But fearing rejection.

Wanting intimacy.
But fearing what intimacy requires.

This creates emotional contradiction.

Some people deeply love others while simultaneously pushing them away emotionally.

Not because they want distance.

But because closeness activates wounds they never healed.

The frightening reality is that prolonged emotional shutdown can slowly harden the heart.

Some people suppress emotions so long they begin losing access to tenderness altogether.

Compassion weakens.
Sensitivity decreases.

Empathy dulls.

And eventually emotional numbness begins feeling normal.

This is spiritually dangerous.

Because God did not create people merely to function mechanically.

He created us:

For connection.
For truth.
For intimacy.
For love.
For honesty.
For relationship.

Silence becomes dangerous when it replaces honesty.

When people hide behind emotional walls long enough, they begin confusing self-protection with peace.

But guardedness is not peace.

Isolation is not healing.

Emotional distance is not strength.

Some people appear calm externally while internally carrying:

- rage
- fear
- torment
- insecurity
- rejection
- shame
- bitterness
- loneliness

The silence simply conceals it.

This is why healing often requires learning vulnerability again.

Not uncontrolled emotional chaos.

But honest emotional openness.

Some wounded people must learn how to:

- communicate honestly
- express emotions safely
- confront conflict maturely
- receive correction without shutting down
- allow themselves to be emotionally seen

Because healing requires exposure.

And exposure terrifies emotionally guarded people.

But walls that keep pain out also keep love out.

The same walls protecting wounded people from rejection often prevent them from experiencing intimacy, healing, peace, and emotional freedom.

Many people are not trapped because healing is unavailable.

They are trapped because silence became safer than honesty.

But silence cannot heal what truth refuses to expose.

And eventually every hidden heart wound begins speaking somehow.

If not through words—

then through distance.

Through anger.
Through control.
Through detachment.
Through emotional absence.
Through sabotage.
Through loneliness.

Or through relationships slowly dying beneath the weight of unspoken pain and emotional absence.

This is why healing begins when wounded people stop hiding behind silence and finally become honest about what is living inside them.

Because emotional honesty is not weakness.

It is courage.

And many people will never become emotionally whole until they stop surviving through silence and start healing through truth and deliverance.

Chapter 12

Performing Healing

Many people know how to imitate healing without ever experiencing healing.

This is one of the most dangerous realities surrounding brokenness.

Because imitation can look convincing.

A person may learn the language of healing while remaining deeply wounded internally.

They know what to say.
How to sound mature.
How to sound spiritual.
How to sound emotionally aware.

But language alone does not transform the soul.

Many wounded people become experts at performance because performance feels safer than exposure.

True healing requires honesty.

Performance only requires presentation.

And presentation is easier.

It is easier to appear healed than to confront the darkness living underneath the image.

This is why many broken people become performers.

Performing confidence.
Performing peace.
Performing happiness.
Performing spirituality.
Performing emotional stability.
Performing strength.

But performance cannot free the soul.

Some people know how to appear emotionally healthy publicly while privately battling torment they refuse to confront honestly.

Others know how to appear spiritually mature while remaining deeply controlled by pride, lust, insecurity, fear, bitterness, manipulation, rage, or hidden emotional wounds.

The frightening reality is that brokenness can become highly functional.

A person can:
- lead
- teach
- preach
- build businesses
- motivate others
- serve faithfully
- remain internally fractured

Because activity is not transformation.

Noise is not healing.

Emotion is not deliverance.

Some people cry during worship services yet remain unchanged because emotional moments alone do not heal what pride still protects.

Others become deeply involved in religion not because they are free, but because religious activity helps them avoid confronting themselves honestly.

Religion can become a hiding place for wounded people.

Not genuine intimacy with God.

Religious performance.

Some people use:

- ministry
- church attendance
- scripture knowledge
- spiritual language
- public serving
- leadership positions
- outward holiness

to avoid confronting unresolved emotional and spiritual brokenness within themselves.

They know how to look transformed without actually becoming transformed.

This is why some people can quote scripture while remaining emotionally toxic.

Some preach forgiveness while secretly feeding bitterness.
Some speak constantly about love while controlling everyone around them.
Some appear humble publicly while privately consumed with pride and insecurity.
Some worship passionately while secretly battling lust, sexual immorality, manipulation, rage, fear, or emotional instability.

The performance creates illusion.

And illusion becomes dangerous because eventually both the individual and everyone around them begin believing healing has already occurred.

But pretending to be healed is not the same as becoming healed.

A person can imitate peace while internally living in torment.

Imitate confidence while secretly drowning in insecurity.
Imitate spiritual maturity while remaining emotionally immature.
Imitate intimacy with God while avoiding genuine surrender.

Many people have learned how to manage appearances rather than pursue freedom.

Why?

Because freedom requires exposure.

And exposure terrifies wounded people.

Some people secretly fear that if others truly saw what was happening inside them, they would be rejected.

So they maintain the image.

The image becomes survival.

The strong image.
The spiritual image.
The successful image.
The emotionally stable image.
The independent image.

But images become exhausting to maintain.

Many people are emotionally tired because pretending requires constant effort.

Constant monitoring.
Constant protection.
Constant self-preservation.

The person becomes trapped inside the version of themselves they created for others to see.

And eventually they no longer know who they really are beneath the performance.

This is one reason many people feel empty despite external success.

The external image may appear impressive.

But the soul knows the truth.

The soul knows when peace is fake.

The soul knows when confidence is built on insecurity.

The soul knows when spirituality is performance instead of relationship.

The soul knows when the person is surviving rather than living freely.

This is why many high-functioning individuals secretly battle anxiety, emptiness, depression, addiction, fear, loneliness, and emotional exhaustion despite appearing successful externally.

Performance cannot sustain the human soul forever.

Eventually hidden brokenness begins leaking into behavior.

Sometimes through anger.
Sometimes through addictions.
Sometimes through pride.
Sometimes through emotional shutdown.
Sometimes through secret sin.
Sometimes through manipulation.
Sometimes through control.

Sometimes through relationships collapsing beneath unresolved wounds.

What remains hidden eventually speaks.

Even if words never do.

This is why genuine healing requires truth.

Not partial truth.

Complete truth.

Truth about wounds.
Truth about fears.
Truth about pride.
Truth about insecurity.
Truth about addictions.
Truth about emotional brokenness.
Truth about hidden motives.
Truth about hidden pain.

Healing cannot occur where honesty is absent.

Many wounded people desperately want freedom while simultaneously resisting the exposure freedom requires.

They want:

- Peace without surrender
- Healing without humility
- Transformation without honesty
- Freedom without vulnerability

But hidden things survive in darkness.

And darkness protects bondage.

This is why many people remain trapped for years despite constantly surrounding themselves with spiritual activity.

They hear sermons.
Read books.
Attend conferences.
Serve faithfully.

Listen to podcasts.
Study scripture.

Yet never truly change.

Because information alone cannot heal what pride refuses to expose.

Some people become spiritually educated prisoners.

Knowledge increases.

But freedom never comes.

Because freedom requires more than awareness.

It requires surrender.

Many wounded people know exactly why they behave the way they do.

They understand:
- their trauma
- their abandonment
- their rejection
- their emotional wounds
- their insecurities

But understanding pain is not the same as becoming free from it.

Freedom requires allowing God to confront the places performance has hidden.

This is why healing often feels terrifying.

Because healing dismantles false identities.

The person who built their identity around appearing strong must confront weakness.

The person who built their identity around control must learn surrender.

The person who built their identity around emotional distance must learn vulnerability.

The person who built their identity around religious performance must learn intimacy with God beyond image management.

Healing strips away masks.

And masks rarely come off comfortably.

Many people fear exposure more than bondage.

So they remain trapped inside carefully constructed versions of themselves.

Versions designed to look healed while still bleeding internally.

But eventually the soul becomes exhausted from pretending.

This is often where healing finally begins.

Not when the person becomes impressive.

But when they become honest.

Honest enough to stop performing.

Honest enough to stop hiding.
Honest enough to admit: "I am not as free as I pretend to be."

That moment of honesty becomes the beginning of transformation.

Because God cannot heal the version of a person they are pretending to be.

He heals the real person underneath the performance.

The wounded person.
The fearful person.
The prideful person.
The insecure person.
The exhausted person.
The broken person hiding behind the image.

This is why true healing requires more than emotional experiences or outward activity.

It requires surrendering the performance entirely.

Because healing begins where pretending ends.

Chapter 13

Why Healing Feels Threatening

Many wounded people do not resist healing because they enjoy suffering.

They resist healing because healing threatens the identity they built around survival.

Brokenness changes people.

Not only emotionally.

But psychologically.
Relationally.
Spiritually.
Internally.

Over time many wounded individuals slowly build entire versions of themselves around self-protection.

The angry person learns anger creates distance.

The emotionally detached person learns vulnerability feels unsafe.

The controlling person learns control creates temporary security.

The prideful person learns image protection hides insecurity.

The silent person learns emotional withdrawal prevents exposure.

These survival mechanisms may begin as protection.

But eventually they become identity.

The person no longer says:
"I developed this because I was wounded."

Now they say:
"This is just who I am."

That sentence has imprisoned countless people emotionally and spiritually.

Because once dysfunction becomes identity, healing begins feeling dangerous.

Why?

Because healing would require dismantling the version of themselves they spent years building.

And that process feels terrifying.

Many wounded people secretly fear:

- vulnerability
- exposure
- accountability
- surrender
- intimacy
- emotional honesty
- dependence
- being fully seen

Some fear rejection so deeply that they keep everyone emotionally distant.

Others fear losing control.

Others fear what they may discover if they finally stop running from themselves.

This is why some people sabotage healing the moment healing becomes possible.

A healthy relationship suddenly feels uncomfortable.

A peaceful environment feels unfamiliar.

An emotionally safe person feels suspicious.

Why?

Because brokenness becomes familiar.

And familiar things often feel safer than healthy things to wounded individuals.

Some people grew up surrounded by chaos for so long that peace now feels emotionally unnatural.

Others were raised around manipulation so consistently that healthy communication feels weak or strange.

Others were wounded so deeply by rejection that genuine love feels unbelievable.

Brokenness conditions people to survive unhealthy environments.

Eventually they begin feeling emotionally "at home" inside dysfunction.

This is one reason many wounded people repeatedly enter destructive relationships.

Not because they consciously desire pain.

But because pain feels recognizable.

And recognizable feels safe.

Healing threatens those patterns.

Because healing introduces unfamiliar territory.

Truth.

Peace.
Honesty.
Stability.
Vulnerability.
Intimacy.
Gratitude.
Humility.

All of these feel threatening to wounded individuals who built survival around emotional protection.

This is why some people become defensive when confronted lovingly.

The confrontation threatens the image.

Others become angry.
Others withdraw emotionally.
Others blame everyone around them.
Others mock truth entirely.

Because brokenness fights exposure.

Many people want relief from pain while refusing the surrender healing requires.

They want peace without honesty.

Freedom without exposure.

Healing without accountability.

Transformation without vulnerability.

But true healing cannot coexist with deception.

Hidden things survive in darkness.

This is why wounded people often fear transparency.

Transparency removes hiding places.

It exposes masks.

It confronts false identities.

It forces honesty.

And honesty terrifies brokenness.

Some people would rather remain dysfunctional than become exposed.

Not because they are evil.

But because survival convinced them vulnerability is dangerous.

Some learned:

- never trust fully
- never depend emotionally
- never admit weakness
- never expose pain
- never let people too close

Eventually survival mode becomes permanent.

And the person no longer knows how to function without walls.

Walls of pride.
Walls of silence.
Walls of control.
Walls of independence.
Walls of emotional distance.

But walls protecting wounded people from pain also prevent

intimacy, peace, and healing from reaching them.

This is why healing often feels emotionally violent internally.

Not because healing destroys people.

But because healing destroys false versions of people.

The false strong version.
The false invulnerable version.
The false independent version.
The false spiritually mature version.
The false emotionally unaffected version.

Healing confronts illusion.

And illusions rarely collapse comfortably.

Many people secretly fear who they will become without the wounds they built their identity around.

Who are they without the anger?

Without the pride?
Without the emotional walls?
Without the control?
Without the survival mechanisms?

Some people no longer know.

This is why brokenness often clings to familiarity even when familiarity is destroying the person.

Because brokenness fears uncertainty more than suffering.

But healing requires stepping into unfamiliar territory.

Trusting again.
Feeling again.
Being honest again.
Connecting again.
Allowing vulnerability again.
Allowing God to confront hidden places again.

This process can feel terrifying for wounded individuals because healing requires surrendering control.

And control became their emotional safety.

But healing cannot fully enter places still ruled by self-protection.

This is why many people remain trapped for years.

Not because God is unwilling to heal them.

But because brokenness convinced them hiding is safer than honesty.

Yet eventually the exhaustion of surviving becomes heavier than the fear of healing.

This is often where transformation begins.

Not when the person becomes fearless.

But when they become willing.

Willing to stop pretending.
Willing to stop hiding.

Willing to stop protecting the wounds.
Willing to finally confront what has been living inside them for years.

Healing begins when truth becomes more important than image protection.

And freedom begins the moment wounded people stop running from the very thing God is trying to heal by delivering from the bondage they are in.

Chapter 14
Healed and Whole

There are people who have been healed.

Not perfect people.
Not people who never struggled.
Not people who never carried wounds.

But people who finally stopped hiding long enough for God to transform them.

Wholeness exists.
Peace exists.
Freedom exists.

Not temporary emotional relief.
Not religious performance.
Not image management.

Real freedom.

The kind where a person no longer needs pride to feel safe.
The kind where anger no longer controls every reaction.
The kind where fear no longer dominates every decision.
The kind where emotional walls no longer prevent intimacy.
The kind where truth replaces deception.

Many wounded people secretly believe healing is impossible for them.

Some have carried pain for decades.

Others survived rejection, abandonment, betrayal, trauma, abuse, shame, addiction, emotional neglect, or spiritual bondage for so long that brokenness now feels permanent.

But brokenness is not identity.

Pain may influence a person.

But it does not have to define them forever.

Healing begins when people finally stop protecting what is destroying them.

Many people spend years asking God to remove pain while continuing to protect the pride, fear, bitterness, unforgiveness, control, lust, manipulation, or emotional walls connected to that pain.

But healing requires surrender.
Not partial surrender.
Complete surrender.

God cannot transform masks.

He transforms with truth.

This is why genuine healing begins with honesty.

Honesty about:
- heart wounds
- fears
- pride
- insecurity
- emotional brokenness
- hidden sin

- hidden pain
- hidden rage
- hidden shame

Healing begins when the person finally admits:
"I am not okay."

For many wounded people those words become the first true step toward freedom.

Because pretending ends. And truth begins.

Many people have lived so long performing strength that honesty feels terrifying.
But healing grows in honesty.

Not performance.

This is why humility becomes essential.

Humility tears down self-protection.
Humility allows accountability.
Humility allows correction.
Humility allows vulnerability.
Humility allows God to expose what pride tried to conceal.

Many wounded people remain trapped because they confuse healing with emotional experiences.

But healing is deeper than feelings.

Healing transforms:
- thinking
- identity

- relationships
- reactions
- desires
- emotional patterns
- spiritual perception

Healing changes:

How a person loves.
How they communicate.
How they respond to conflict.
How they handle correction.
How they see themselves.
How they see others.
How they see God.

A healed person no longer constantly needs validation to feel valuable.

They no longer manipulate others emotionally to feel secure.
They no longer need control to feel safe.
They no longer need masks to survive intimacy.

Healing does not make people emotionless.

It makes them free.

Free to love honestly.
Free to communicate honestly.
Free to be vulnerable without collapsing internally.
Free to receive correction without defensiveness.
Free to apologize sincerely.
Free to forgive.
Free to trust God beyond fear.

Many healed people still carry memories of what wounded them.

But the wounds no longer control them.

The trauma no longer defines identity.
The rejection no longer dictates worth.
The fear no longer controls decisions.
The bitterness no longer poisons relationships.

This is the difference between surviving and becoming whole.

Surviving keeps people alive.

Wholeness makes people free.

This is why healed people often carry peace that broken people cannot understand.

Not because healed people never suffered.

But because they stopped building identity around suffering.

Some wounded people become addicted to victimhood.

Others addicted to chaos.
Others addicted to emotional instability.
Others addicted to self-protection.

But healed people eventually realize freedom requires responsibility.

Responsibility for:
- thoughts
- reactions
- choices
- healing
- boundaries
- honesty
- surrender

Healing also requires forgiveness.

Not because what happened was acceptable.

But because unforgiveness chains wounded people emotionally and spiritually to the very pain they are trying to escape.

Forgiveness does not always remove memories immediately.

But it breaks agreement with bitterness.

And bitterness silently poisons the soul.

Many people remain emotionally exhausted because they are carrying years of unresolved pain God never intended them to continue carrying.

Wholeness requires release.

Release of:
- pride
- shame
- fear
- control
- bitterness
- hidden sin
- false identities

This is why healing often feels like death internally.

Because the false version of the person begins collapsing.

The version built around survival.
The version built around pride.
The version built around image protection.
The version built around emotional walls.

But what dies in healing is not the real person.

It is the prison.

And many people spend years defending prisons they secretly hate living inside.

Freedom begins when the walls finally come down.

When honesty replaces pretending.
When surrender replaces control.
When humility replaces pride.
When truth replaces illusion.
When intimacy with God becomes greater than maintaining appearances.

Some people fear they have been broken too long to become whole.

But God specializes in restoring what people believed could never heal.

He restores:

- identities
- minds
- relationships
- emotions
- hearts
- souls

The person who once lived in fear can become peaceful.
The person who once lived in rage can become gentle.
The person who once lived emotionally shut down can become emotionally healthy.
The person once trapped in shame can become secure.
The person once controlled by heart wounds can become free.

Wholeness does not mean the person never struggles again.

It means brokenness no longer rules them.

This book was never written to shame wounded people.

It was written to expose hidden brokenness so healing could begin.

Because what remains hidden remains empowered.

But what is exposed to truth can finally become free.

Many people are not evil.

They are wounded.

Not beyond hope.

Just hidden beneath layers of pain, pride, fear, survival, and deception.

But healing is possible.
Freedom is possible.
Wholeness is possible.

And the moment a person finally becomes honest enough to stop pretending—

Transformation begins.

And Transformation leads to seeking out Deliverance.

And Deliverance leads to Inner Healing.

And Inner Healing leads to becoming Healed and Whole.

****** Thank you kindly for your purchase and for reading this! ******

Lastly, if you don't have **<u>SALVATION</u>** (accepted what Jesus Christ did for you on the cross), but you want it, then believe and repeat the following prayer out loud to God wherever you are.

Father, I thank you for sending Jesus to die for me on the cross, be buried and then rise up on the 3rd day with all power in heaven and earth. Please forgive me of all of my sins and unrighteousness and I repent for all of my sins and unrighteousness. Please cleanse me now and fill me with your Holy Spirit.

It is because of that, I accept what you did for me and now Jesus Christ is my Lord and Saviour.

Visit:

www.tomenterprisesllc.com

To join my mail list and keep up with my latest releases, speaking engagements and other pertinent events and information.

BE SURE TO GET THE WORKBOOK FOR SELF EVAL

***** PLEASE REMEMBER TO LEAVE A REVIEW *****

The following are great reads I recommend to help deepen understanding of the demonic realm, demonic possession and influence and how they operate. It will also bring understanding to what Inner Healing & Deliverance looks like.

It's not in any particular order except for #1, after that its random:

1. The BIBLE
2. Soul Ties, By Frank Hammond
3. The Bondage Breaker, By Neil Anderson
4. The Screwtape Letters, By C S Lewis
5. Clean House, Strong House, By Kimberly Daniels
6. Deliverance From Demonic Covenants & Curses, By Rev. James A. Solomon
7. They Shall Expel Demons, By Derek Prince
8. Pigs In The Parlor, By Frank Hammond
9. Obstacles To Deliverance, By Frank Hammond
10. Understanding Spiritual Warfare: A Comprehensive Guide, By Sam Storms
11. How To Cast Out Demons, By Isaiah Saldivar

For TRUE ***INNER HEALING & DELIVERANCE,***
virtual or in-person, visit:

LIONHEART CHURCH
3771 Floyd Rd
Austell, GA 30106
404-282-6400
Pastors: OTHA & LaRONNA TURNBOUGH

www.lionheartchurch.org

www.ingramcontent.com/pod-product-compliance
Lightning Source LLC
La Vergne TN
LVHW040520210926
848480LV00007BA/1524
* 9 7 9 8 9 9 6 5 8 1 5 1 1 *